Family Circle

GREAT CHICKEN RECIPES

Edited by Patricia Curtis

Designed by Ronald Gilbert

 COWLES

Cowles Education Corporation

President and Editor: David C. Whitney
Executive Editor: Francine Klagsbrun
Art Director: Ronald Gilbert
Senior Editor, Family Circle Books: Patricia Curtis
Production Manager: Robert F. Hirsch

With acknowledgments to National Broiler Council,
Poultry & Egg National Board, Associated Pimiento
Canners, and Delmarva Poultry Industry.

CONTENTS

PREFACE

Everybody likes chicken. It can be a family dish, wholesome and homey, or it can be dressed up with all kinds of delicacies in an elaborate gourmet dish. Chicken is tasty, nourishing, inexpensive, and easily available everywhere. Chicken appeals to weight-worriers because of its low calorie count, yet homemakers like it for family meals because it is a high-protein energy food. And, as the appetizing kitchen-tested recipes in this book show, chicken can be prepared by every known cooking method.

Here, then, are chicken dishes in many different roles—at family meals, at company dinners, at tables around the world, on barbecue grills, and in picnic baskets. The recipes have been chosen to inspire the experienced cook and encourage the novice. Enjoy!

The Editors

Basic Fried Chicken

FRIED CHICKEN

Fried chicken is perhaps the all-round family favorite. It has special appeal to youngsters because it can be — and usually is — eaten with the fingers. That's one good reason why it should be crisp and well drained. Another virtue of fried chicken is that it tastes good piping hot, lukewarm, or refrigerator-cold. If it's fried chicken for a picnic you have in mind, be sure to check the recipes for Dunking Chicken in the PICNIC CHICK section, and Herb-Fried Drumsticks in the section on CHICKEN FOR A CROWD.

GINGER CRISP CHICKEN

Secret of this favorite is double cooking: first baking, then frying. The ginger in the golden crust gives it a slightly spicy flavor.

Bake at 350° for 1 hour.

Makes 6 servings.

2 broiler-fryers (about 2 pounds each), cut in serving-size pieces
2 teaspoons salt
1 teaspoon rosemary
1/2 cup water
1 1/2 cups Ginger Batter
Shortening or salad oil for frying

1. Wash chicken pieces; pat dry. Place in a single layer in a large shallow baking pan; sprinkle with salt and rosemary; add water; cover.
2. Bake in moderate oven (350°) 1 hour.
3. While chicken cooks, prepare Ginger Batter (see right).
4. Remove chicken from pan; pull off skin and remove small rib bones, if you wish; drain chicken thoroughly on paper toweling.
5. Melt enough shortening or pour in enough salad oil to make a depth of 2 inches in a large frying pan or electric deep-fat fryer. Heat until hot (350° in electric fryer).
6. Dip chicken pieces, 2 or 3 at a time, into Ginger Batter; hold over bowl to let excess drip back.
7. Fry in hot shortening 3 minutes, or until golden-brown. Lift out with a slotted spoon; drain well. Keep warm on a hot platter, covered with foil, until all pieces are cooked.

GINGER BATTER

Makes about 1 1/2 cups.

1 1/4 cups sifted regular flour
1 teaspoon baking powder
1 teaspoon salt
1/2 teaspoon ground ginger
1 egg
1 cup milk
1/4 cup salad oil

1. Sift flour, baking powder, salt, and ginger into a medium-size bowl.
2. Add remaining ingredients all at once; beat with a rotary beater until smooth.

9

SOUTHERN FRIED CHICKEN

Time-honored, trusty, crusty chicken with cream gravy.

Makes 6 servings.

2 broiler-fryers (about 2 pounds each), cut up
3 cups light cream or table cream
2 cups plus 1 tablespoon sifted flour
2½ teaspoons salt
½ teaspoon pepper
Shortening or vegetable oil

1. Wash chicken pieces; pat dry. Place in a single layer in a large shallow dish; pour 1 cup of the cream over top; chill at least 20 minutes.

2. Shake chicken pieces, a few at a time, in a mixture of the 2 cups flour, 2 teaspoons salt, and ¼ teaspoon pepper in a paper bag to coat well. Dip each again in remaining cream in dish; shake again in flour mixture. (Double coating gives chicken its thick crisp crust.)

3. Melt enough shortening or pour enough vegetable oil into each of two large heavy frying pans to make a depth of 1½ inches; heat. Add chicken pieces, skin side down. Brown slowly, turning once, then continue cooking 30 minutes, or until crisp and tender. Remove to a heated serving platter; keep warm while making gravy.

4. Pour all drippings from frying pans into a small bowl; measure 2 tablespoonfuls and return to one pan. Stir in 1 tablespoon of flour, remaining ½ teaspoon salt, and ¼ teaspoon pepper. Cook, stirring constantly, until bubbly. Stir in remaining 2 cups cream; continue cooking and stirring, scraping brown bits from bottom of pan, until gravy thickens and boils 1 minute. Serve separately.

BASIC FRIED CHICKEN

Essential to any good cook's repertoire, this chicken can't be hurried — but it is worth waiting for.

Makes 4 servings.

1 broiler-fryer (about 3 pounds)
½ cup flour
1 teaspoon salt
⅛ teaspoon pepper
1 cup bacon drippings or part drippings and shortening

1. Cut chicken into 8 serving-size pieces — 2 breasts, 2 wings, 2 thighs, 2 drumsticks. (Simmer bony back pieces to make broth for gravy, if you wish.) Wash chicken, but do not dry. This is important so skin will take on a thick flour coating.

2. Mix flour, salt, and pepper in a bag. Shake pieces, a few at a time, to coat evenly all over.

3. Heat bacon drippings ¼-inch deep in a large heavy frying pan on medium heat, or in an electric skillet to 360°. Arrange chicken, without crowding, in a single layer in hot fat.

4. Brown slowly for 15 minutes. When pink juices start to show on top, turn and brown the other side 15 minutes. Slow cooking, plus turning just once, gives the chicken its crisp coating.

5. When pieces are browned, pile all back into pan or skillet and cover. Lower range heat to simmer or reset control at 260°. Let chicken cook 20 minutes longer, or until it's richly golden and fork-tender.

GOLDEN-COATED FRIED CHICKEN

Bread the chicken pieces and chill them, then fry very slowly — this gives the crusty golden coat.

Makes 6 servings.

2 broiler-fryers (about 2 pounds each), cut in serving-size pieces
1 cup (8-ounce carton) sour cream
2 tablespoons lemon juice
1 teaspoon salt
1 teaspoon garlic salt
1 teaspoon Worcestershire sauce
1¼ cups fine dry bread crumbs
Shortening or vegetable oil for frying
1 package chicken gravy mix

1. Wash chicken pieces; pat dry.
2. Mix sour cream, lemon juice, salt, garlic salt, and Worcestershire sauce in a small bowl; place bread crumbs in a pie plate. Brush chicken pieces with sour cream mixture, then roll in crumbs to coat well.
3. Place in a single layer on a cookie sheet. Chill at least 1 hour. Chill remaining sour cream mixture for Step 6.
4. Melt enough shortening or pour in enough vegetable oil to make ½-inch depth in a large frying pan.
5. Brown chicken, a few pieces at a time, very slowly in hot fat; return all pieces to pan; cover. Cook over *very low* heat 30 minutes, or until chicken is tender.
6. Prepare chicken gravy mix, following label directions. Stir ¼ cup of the hot gravy into remaining sour cream mixture; stir back into remaining gravy in pan; heat slowly just until hot. Serve separately to spoon over chicken.

COUNTRY FRIED CHICKEN

Chicken the way it was served down on the farm in Grandma's day (if you were lucky). It's crisp and flavory, with gravy.

Makes 6 to 8 servings.

2 broiler-fryers (about 2 pounds each), cut into serving-size pieces
⅔ cup flour
2 teaspoons salt
1 teaspoon paprika
¼ teaspoon pepper
1 cup bacon drippings
2 cloves garlic
1 bay leaf
2 cups Milk Gravy

1. Wash and dry chicken pieces. Shake, a few at a time, in mixture of flour, salt, paprika, and pepper in paper bag to coat thoroughly.
2. Heat bacon drippings with whole cloves of garlic and bay leaf in large frying pan.
3. Place chicken in single layer in hot drippings. (Do not crowd as pieces should have enough room to brown without touching each other.) Cook slowly, turning once or twice to brown both sides. (It will take about 30 minutes.)
4. Return all chicken to frying pan; cover; cook slowly 20 minutes, or until tender. Uncover; cook 5 minutes longer to crisp coating. Remove chicken to heated platter; keep hot in slow oven long enough to make Milk Gravy.

MILK GRAVY: Tip pan and pour off all drippings into a cup, leaving crusty brown bits in pan. (Be sure to remove garlic cloves and bay leaf.) Return 3 tablespoons drippings to pan; blend in 3 tablespoons flour; cook, stirring all the time, just until mixture bubbles. Stir in 1 cup water and 1 cup milk slowly; continue cooking and stirring, scraping brown bits from bottom and sides of pan, until gravy thickens and boils 1 minute. Season to taste with salt. Makes about 2 cups.

11

Little Chicken Roasts

ROAST CHICKEN

Of all chicken dishes, roast chicken has the most eye-appeal, and no wonder, for a perfectly roasted, golden-brown juicy whole chicken is a beautiful sight. Most people stuff their roast chickens; if you use one of the delicious stuffings with the roast chicken recipes here (or one from the section on STUFFINGS), remember to pack it lightly into the chicken, for stuffing swells as it cooks. For some handy, illustrated advice about roast chicken, see the section How TO STUFF AND TRUSS A CHICKEN; a roasting timetable is included.

For some fancy roast chicken dishes, look in the "COMPANY'S COMING" section and in CHICKEN SOUTH-OF-THE-BORDER.

GLAZED CHICKEN WITH PEACHES

A mouth-watering masterpiece of glossy little roasters on a bed of rice with golden peaches.

Roast at 375° for 1½ to 2 hours.
Makes 6 servings.

2 roasting chickens (about 3½ pounds each)
1 teaspoon salt
2 cups stuffing
2 tablespoons melted butter or margarine
Golden Glaze and Golden Peaches

1. Wash and dry chickens; sprinkle inside with salt; stuff neck and body cavities lightly with stuffing. (Savory Stuffing is good with this chicken; for recipe, turn to the section on STUFFINGS.) Skewer neck skin to body, close body cavity and tie legs to tailpiece; place chickens on rack in shallow roasting pan; brush with melted butter or margarine.
2. Roast in moderate oven (375°) 1½ to 2 hours (figure roasting time at 30 minutes per pound for one bird), or until drumstick moves easily at joint.
3. About 20 minutes before chickens are done, brush with Golden Glaze; continue roasting (brush once more after 10 minutes) until chickens are done.
4. Serve on a bed of rice on a heated platter, garnished with Golden Peaches.

GOLDEN GLAZE AND GOLDEN PEACHES

Bake at 375° for 20 minutes.

1 can (about 1 pound) peach halves
2 tablespoons bottled meat sauce

1. Drain peach halves, saving syrup in small bowl; arrange peaches, cut side up, in shallow baking dish.
2. Blend meat sauce into syrup for Golden Glaze and brush over chickens; brush peach halves with rest of glaze for Golden Peaches; bake peaches in oven along with chicken during last 20 minutes of roasting time.

SAVORY ROAST CHICKEN

Attention beginners: you almost can't muff this one. Look for the good-buy young roasters, heavy with meat on their frames.

Roast at 375° about 2 hours.
Makes 4 servings.

1 roasting chicken (about 4 pounds)
$\frac{1}{2}$ teaspoon salt
2 cups Savory Stuffing
1 to 2 tablespoons butter or margarine

1. Wash chicken and pat dry. Sprinkle inside with salt.
2. Stuff neck and body cavities lightly with Savory Stuffing (bake any remaining stuffing in a casserole). Skewer neck skin to body, secure body cavity closed, and tie legs to tailpiece.
3. Place chicken on rack in shallow roasting pan; rub with butter or margarine. Roast at 375° about 2 hours (figure time at 30 minutes per pound), or until drumstick moves easily at joint.

SAVORY STUFFING

Makes 2 cups.

$\frac{1}{2}$ cup chopped celery leaves
2 tablespoons chopped onion
4 tablespoons ($\frac{1}{2}$ stick) butter or margarine
$\frac{1}{2}$ cup water
2 cups ready-mix bread stuffing ($\frac{1}{2}$ of an 8-ounce package)

1. Sauté celery leaves and onion in butter or margarine in medium-size saucepan. Add water; heat to boiling.
2. Stir in bread stuffing; toss with fork just until moistened.

ROAST CAPON

This elegant fowl should be simply prepared so as not to detract from its own fine flavor.

Roast at 325° about 2½ hours.
Makes 6 servings.

1 ready-to-cook capon (about 7 pounds)
Salt
Pepper
6 cups stuffing
Melted butter or margarine

1. Sprinkle chicken inside with salt and pepper.
2. Pack stuffing lightly into neck cavity. (Bread-and-Butter Stuffing is good with capon; for recipe, see section on STUFFINGS.) Smooth neck skin over stuffing and fasten with wooden picks or skewers to back of bird; twist wing tips until they rest flat against fastened neck skin.
3. Stuff body cavity lightly; fasten opening, and tie legs together and fasten to tailpiece.
4. Place capon, breast side up, on rack in a large open roasting pan; brush well with melted butter or margarine; cover breast with double-thick cheesecloth moistened with additional fat.
5. Roast in slow oven (325°) 2½ hours, or until meaty part of drumstick is tender when pierced with a 2-tine fork; baste frequently during roasting.
6. Place capon on heated serving platter and serve while hot.

Quick and Easy TWIN STUFFED CHICKENS

To a new cook in a hurry: use small broilers and stuffing mix to.put dinner on the table sooner. Roast at 375° for 1¼ hours. Makes 4 to 6 servings.

2 whole broiler-fryers (2½ pounds each)
Seasoned salt
1 cup chopped celery
1 small onion, chopped (¼ cup)
6 tablespoons butter or margarine
⅔ cup water
2 cups ready-mix bread stuffing

1. Rinse chickens; pat dry; sprinkle inside with seasoned salt.
2. In a medium-size frying pan, sauté celery and onion in 4 tablespoons of the butter or margarine until soft. Stir in water and stuffing mix until mixture is evenly moist.
3. Stuff lightly into neck and body cavities of chickens; place in a roasting pan. Rub chickens with remaining 2 tablespoons butter or margarine.
4. Roast in moderate oven (375°) for 1¼ hours, or until tender.

LITTLE CHICKEN ROASTS

When you plan to make this delicious recipe, remember that everyone rates a half chicken and a portion of stuffing.
Roast at 375° for 1½ hours.
Makes 6 servings.

3 whole broiler-fryers (1½ pounds each)
½ cup (1 stick) butter or margarine
1 can (about 9 ounces) crushed pineapple
3 cups soft bread crumbs (6 slices)
½ cup flaked coconut
½ cup chopped celery
½ teaspoon salt
¼ teaspoon poultry seasoning
2 tablespoons bottled steak sauce
Sweet-and-Sour Sauce

1. Rinse chickens inside and out with cold water; drain, then pat dry. Sprinkle inside with salt.
2. Melt butter or margarine in a small saucepan. Drain syrup from pineapple into a cup and set aside for Step 6.
3. Combine pineapple with bread crumbs, coconut, and celery in a medium-size bowl; drizzle 4 tablespoons of the melted butter or margarine over; toss with a fork until crumbs are lightly coated. (Save remaining butter or margarine for Step 5.)
4. Stuff neck and body cavities of chickens lightly with pineapple-bread mixture.

Smooth neck skin over stuffing and skewer to back; close body cavity and tie legs to tail. Place chickens in a roasting pan.
5. Stir salt and poultry seasoning into saved 4 tablespoons butter or margarine in saucepan; brush part over chickens.
6. Roast 1 hour in moderate oven (375°), basting several times with butter mixture. Stir saved pineapple syrup and steak sauce into any remaining butter in saucepan; brush generously over chickens.
7. Continue roasting, basting once or twice more, 30 minutes longer, or until drumsticks move easily and meaty part of thigh feels soft.
8. Remove chickens to heated serving platter; keep warm while making sauce.
9. When ready to serve, cut away strings from chickens. Garnish platter with water cress and preserved mixed fruits, if you wish. Pass sauce in a separate bowl.

SWEET-AND-SOUR SAUCE: Blend 2 tablespoons cornstarch into drippings in roasting pan; stir in 1 cup water. Cook, stirring all the time, just until mixture thickens and boils 3 minutes. Stir in 2 tablespoons brown sugar and 1 tablespoon lemon juice. Strain into heated serving bowl. Makes about 1¼ cups.

Baked Chicken Parmesan

BAKED CHICKEN

When it comes to ease of preparation, baked chicken dishes probably take the prize. You simply season or coat chicken parts with something good, put them in the oven, and go about your business for about an hour. Then, there's your main dish for dinner — sizzling and savory.

If you want an elegant baked chicken dish, try Chicken Perfection, Baked Chicken with Wine, or one of the other aristocrats in the "COMPANY'S COMING" section. For baked chicken casseroles, see CASSEROLES. And you will find some exotic baked chicken recipes in CHICKEN SOUTH-OF-THE-BORDER and in CONTINENTAL CHICKEN.

BAKED CHICKEN PARMESAN

An easy and pleasing variation of the beloved Italian veal dish. This time it's chicken that's flavored with piquant Parmesan cheese.

Bake at 425° about 50 minutes.
Makes 8 servings.

¹/₃ cup salad oil
2 broiler-fryers, cut in serving-size pieces
1 teaspoon oregano
1 teaspoon salt
Paprika
1 can (3 or 4 ounces) sliced mushrooms
    OR ¹/₂ pound fresh mushrooms
3 tablespoons grated Parmesan cheese

1. Line a shallow baking pan with aluminum foil. Pour salad oil into pan. Place in hot oven (425°) to heat, about 10 minutes. Remove pan from oven.
2. Place chicken pieces, skin side down, in hot oil. Sprinkle with half the oregano and salt. Sprinkle lightly with paprika. Return to oven and bake 30 minutes.

3. Turn chicken pieces; sprinkle with remaining oregano and salt, and lightly with paprika. Bake 15 minutes longer; remove from oven.
4. Spoon fat and drippings in pan over chicken. Pour mushrooms (with their liquid if using canned) over chicken; sprinkle with Parmesan cheese; bake 5 minutes longer.

17

SAN FERNANDO PEPPER CHICKEN

Seasoned pepper — a spunky blend — flavors this Southwest chicken dish.

Bake at 350° for 1 hour.
Makes 6 servings.

½ cup (1 stick) butter or margarine
2 broiler-fryers (about 2 pounds each), cut
   in serving-size pieces
1½ tablespoons seasoned pepper
2 teaspoons salt
Savory Mushroom Gravy

1. Melt butter or margarine in large shallow baking pan. Roll chicken pieces one at a time in butter to coat well; then arrange, skin side down, in single layer in pan.
2. Combine seasoned pepper and salt in a small cup; sprinkle half evenly over chicken.
3. Bake in moderate oven (350°) 30 minutes; turn; sprinkle remaining seasoning mixture over. Bake 30 minutes longer, or until chicken is tender and lightly browned.
4. Arrange on heated serving platter; keep warm in a slow oven while making gravy. Serve gravy in separate bowl to spoon over chicken.

SAVORY MUSHROOM GRAVY: Pour off all chicken drippings from pan; return ¼ cupful. Stir in 1 can dry cream-of-mushroom soup mix. Blend in 2 cups water. Cook slowly, stirring constantly, 8 to 10 minutes, until thickened. Makes 2 cups.

CHICKEN BAKED WITH BARBECUE SAUCE

Whip the sauce together in no time, spoon it over chicken, pop the dish in the oven, and forget it while it cooks to savory tenderness.

Bake at 400° about 1 hour.
Makes 6 servings.

2 broiler-fryers (about 2 pounds each), cut
   in serving-size pieces
Butter or margarine
Barbecue Sauce

1. Wash chicken pieces; pat dry; remove skin if you wish.
2. Arrange chicken pieces in a single layer in a well-buttered large shallow baking pan.
3. Spoon Barbecue Sauce over chicken so pieces are well coated. (If you have any leftover sauce, it will keep in a covered jar in the refrigerator.)
4. Bake, uncovered, in hot oven (400°) about 1 hour, or until chicken is tender.

BARBECUE SAUCE

Makes 2½ cups.

2 cans (8 ounces each) tomato sauce
1 medium-size onion, chopped (½ cup)
1 clove garlic, minced
¼ cup soy sauce
2 tablespoons sugar
1 teaspoon dry mustard
⅛ teaspoon cayenne

Mix all ingredients in a medium-size bowl.

CHICKEN CORIANDER

This unusual chicken dish has a delight-
fully spicy flavor.

Bake at 350° for 1 hour.
Makes 6 servings.

3 chicken breasts (about 12 ounces each)
4 tablespoons (¹/₂ stick) butter or margarine
1 small onion, grated
1 tablespoon ground coriander
1¹/₂ teaspoons salt
¹/₂ teaspoon chili powder
1 tablespoon lemon juice
Pan Gravy

1. Halve chicken breasts; remove skin, if
you wish; then cut meat in one piece
from bones.
2. Melt butter or margarine in a shallow
baking pan; stir in seasonings.
3. Roll chicken in mixture to coat well,
then arrange in a single layer in same
pan. Bake in moderate oven (350°) 30
minutes; turn.
4. Continue baking, basting several times
with buttery liquid in pan, 30 minutes
longer, or until chicken is tender. Serve
with Pan Gravy (for recipe, turn to section on GRAVIES).

CREAMY BAKED CHICKEN

Two cream soups make the rich gravy;
one also adds flavor to fluffy corn biscuits
on top.

Bake at 350° about 1 hour, then at 450°
about 15 minutes.
Makes 4 servings.

1 broiler-fryer (2¹/₂ to 3¹/₂ pounds), cut in
  serving-size pieces
1 can condensed cream-of-mushroom soup
1 can condensed cream-of-chicken soup
¹/₂ cup plus 3 tablespoons milk
¹/₂ teaspoon ground ginger
1 cup biscuit mix
¹/₄ cup yellow cornmeal
¹/₂ tablespoon finely chopped crystallized
  ginger

1. Cut away small bones from chicken
breasts; remove all skin if you prefer
chicken cooked without it.
2. Arrange chicken pieces in buttered 12-
cup casserole; combine cream-of-mushroom soup, ½ can (½ cup plus 2 tablespoons) cream-of-chicken soup (save the
rest for Step 4), ½ cup milk, and ground
ginger in small bowl; mix well; pour over
chicken pieces in casserole; cover.

3. Bake in moderate oven (350°) 30 minutes; remove cover; stir to mix sauce and
juices from chicken; cover again; bake 30
minutes longer, or until chicken is tender.
Reset oven to hot (450°).
4. Combine biscuit mix, corn meal, and
crystallized ginger in small bowl; mix 3
tablespoons milk with saved cream-of-
chicken soup; stir into biscuit mixture,
mixing lightly.
5. Remove casserole from oven; uncover
casserole and drop dough by spoonfuls
to make 8 mounds in a ring on top of
chicken.
6. Bake in hot oven (450°) about 15 minutes longer, or until biscuits are puffed
and golden-brown.

CURRY GLAZED CHICKEN

The happy blend of curry and marmalade makes this a special-occasion dish.

Bake at 400° for 1 hour.
Makes 8 servings.

2 broiler-fryer chickens, quartered
6 tablespoons (³/₄ stick) butter or
  margarine
1 large onion, chopped (1 cup)
8 slices raw bacon, diced fine
2 tablespoons flour
1 tablespoon curry powder
1 can condensed beef broth
¹/₄ cup marmalade (ginger or orange)
2 tablespoons catsup
2 tablespoons lemon juice

1. Wash chicken quarters; pat dry; remove skin, if you wish.
2. Melt butter or margarine in a large shallow baking pan. Dip chicken in butter to coat both sides; then arrange, meaty side up, in a single layer in same pan.

3. Bake in hot oven (400°) 20 minutes, or until starting to turn golden.
4. While chicken bakes, combine remaining ingredients in a medium-size saucepan; heat, stirring constantly, to boiling, then simmer, stirring often, 15 minutes, or until thick. Spoon about half over chicken to make a thick coating.
5. Continue baking 20 minutes; spoon on rest of glaze. Bake 20 minutes longer, or until chicken is tender and richly glazed.

SMOTHERED CHICKEN

Baked in liquid under cover, chicken makes its own delicious gravy.

Bake at 350° for 1 hour.
Makes 6 servings.

3 broiler-fryers (about 2 pounds each),
  split
²/₃ cup flour
2 teaspoons salt
¹/₄ teaspoon pepper
6 tablespoons (³/₄ stick) butter or
  margarine
1 medium-size onion, chopped (¹/₂ cup)
2¹/₂ cups water

1. Wash chicken halves; pat dry. Shake with mixture of ⅓ cup flour, 1½ teaspoons salt, and pepper in a paper bag to coat evenly.
2. Brown pieces, several at a time, in

butter or margarine in a large frying pan; place in a single layer in a roasting pan.
3. Sauté onion until soft in drippings in frying pan; stir in 1½ cups of the water and remaining ½ teaspoon salt. Heat, stirring constantly, to boiling; pour over chicken; cover.
4. Bake in moderate oven (350°) for 1 hour or until chicken is tender. Remove to a heated serving platter and keep warm in slow oven while making gravy.
5. Blend remaining ⅓ cup flour and 1 cup water until smooth in a 2-cup measure. Heat liquid in roasting pan to boiling; slowly stir in flour mixture. Cook, stirring constantly, until gravy thickens and boils 1 minute. Darken with a few drops bottled gravy coloring, if you wish. Serve separately to spoon over chicken.

ONION DIP CHICKEN

Sharp onion dip gives this crumb-coated chicken a zesty flavor.

Bake at 350° for 1 hour.
Makes 8 servings.

2 broiler-fryers (about 2 pounds each), cut up
1 envelope (2 packets) onion dip mix
1 cup soft bread crumbs (2 slices)
1 teaspoon salt
⅛ teaspoon pepper

1. Remove skin from chicken, if you wish; cut away small bones from breast pieces.
2. Combine dip mix, bread crumbs, salt, and pepper in a paper bag. Shake chicken pieces, a few at a time, in mixture to coat well. Place, not touching, in a single layer in a buttered large shallow baking pan.
3. Bake in moderate oven (350°) 1 hour, or until chicken is tender and richly browned.

CHICKEN DIABLE

The flavor secret: honey, mustard, and curry powder, an oddly delectable blend.

Bake at 375° for 1 hour.
Makes 4 servings.

1 broiler-fryer (about 3 pounds), cut up
4 tablespoons (½ stick) butter or margarine
½ cup honey
¼ cup prepared mustard
1 teaspoon salt
1 teaspoon curry powder

1. Wash chicken pieces; pat dry; remove skin, if you wish.
2. Melt butter or margarine in a shallow baking pan; stir in remaining ingredients. Roll chicken in butter mixture to coat both sides; then arrange, meaty side up, in a single layer in same pan.
3. Bake in moderate oven (375°) 1 hour, or until chicken is tender and richly glazed.

Quick and Easy

CORN-FLAKE CHICKEN

You can give this chicken its corn-flake coating ahead of time and refrigerate it, oven-ready, till you're ready.

Bake at 425° about 45 minutes.
Makes 4 servings, 2 pieces each.

1 broiler-fryer (about 3 pounds), cut into 8 serving pieces
½ cup buttermilk
½ cup packaged corn-flake crumbs
½ cup flour
1 teaspoon salt
1 teaspoon poultry seasoning

4 tablespoons (½ stick) melted butter or margarine

1. Remove chicken skin, if you wish; then dip chicken pieces in buttermilk in shallow pan; coat with mixture of corn-flake crumbs, flour, salt, and poultry seasoning combined in second shallow pan; arrange chicken pieces in single layer in well-buttered baking pan; pour melted butter or margarine over. (This much may be done ahead.)
2. Bake in hot oven (425°) 45 minutes, or until tender.

Quick and Easy   SPANISH RICE CHICKEN BAKE

A packaged mix is your short cut to a fine Castilian dish.

Bake at 350° for 1 hour.
Makes 8 servings.

**2 broiler-fryers (about 3 pounds each),
   quartered**
¹/₄ cup flour
¹/₄ cup salad oil
1¹/₂ cups raw rice
3 cups water
1 envelope Spanish rice seasoning mix
1 large green pepper, cut in 8 rings
1 cup sliced stuffed green olives

1. Shake chicken with flour in paper bag to coat well. Brown, a few pieces at a time, in salad oil in large frying pan; drain on paper toweling.
2. Place rice in a 10-cup shallow baking dish; arrange browned chicken on top.
3. Stir water into chicken drippings in frying pan; blend in Spanish rice seasoning mix; heat to boiling. Pour over chicken and rice; cover.
4. Bake in moderate oven (350°) 30 minutes; uncover and lay green pepper rings and sliced olives on top. Cover and bake 30 minutes longer, or until chicken and rice are tender, and liquid is absorbed.

BAKED CHICKEN ORIENTALE

This chicken has a rich honey-and-soy glaze, at once sweet and sour.

Bake at 350° for 1 hour.
Makes 4 servings.

**1 broiler-fryer (about 3 pounds), cut in
   serving-size pieces**
¹/₂ cup flour
1 teaspoon salt
¹/₄ teaspoon pepper
8 tablespoons (1 stick) butter or margarine
¹/₄ cup honey
¹/₄ cup lemon juice
1 tablespoon soy sauce

1. Wash chicken pieces; drain. Shake in mixture of flour, salt, and pepper in paper bag to coat well.
2. Melt 4 tablespoons of the butter or margarine in a baking dish, 13x9x2; roll chicken pieces, one at a time, in melted butter to coat all over. Place, skin side down, in single layer in baking dish.
3. Bake in moderate oven (350°) for 30 minutes.
4. Melt remaining 4 tablespoons butter or margarine in small saucepan; stir in honey, lemon juice, and soy sauce until well mixed.
5. Turn chicken; pour honey mixture over. Bake, basting several times with syrup and drippings in pan, 30 minutes longer, or until tender and richly glazed.

POTATO-FLAKE CHICKEN

Mashed potato flakes make the coating for oven-crisped chicken.

Bake at 350° for 1½ hours.
Makes 6 servings.

²/₃ cup evaporated milk (from a tall can)
1 teaspoon salt
1 teaspoon mixed Italian herbs
¹/₈ teaspoon pepper
1 envelope (1½ cups) instant mashed
  potato flakes
2 broiler-fryers, cut up (about 2 pounds
  each)
Quick Cream Gravy

1. Pour evaporated milk into a pie plate; stir in salt, Italian herbs, and pepper. Empty mashed potato flakes into a second pie plate.
2. Dip chicken pieces into evaporated milk mixture, then into potato flakes to coat well. Place in single layer on ungreased cooky sheet.
3. Bake in moderate oven (350°) 1½ hours or until tender and golden brown.
4. Serve with Quick Cream Gravy (for recipe, turn to section on GRAVIES).

Potato-Flake Chicken

23

Perfect Chicken Barbecue

BARBECUED CHICKEN

Barbecuing means cooking on a grill over a very hot fire — usually glowing charcoal. You may fashion a makeshift barbecue pit at the beach, or you may have a stone or brick barbecue built in your backyard. Most people, however, use one of the many types of portable barbecue grills that can be carried or rolled to the site of your feast.

Rotisserie cooking — that is, on a revolving spit over high heat — is also considered barbecuing, for while the apparatus is different, the results you get with the meat are deliciously similar. Most rotisserie cooking today is done with an electric spit over charcoal or electric heat.

Here you will find recipes for chicken both grilled and spitted, sauced and marinated. For bonus barbecue sauces, see also the section on GRAVIES, SAUCES, AND GLAZES.

CINNAMON GLAZED CHICKEN

Savory cinnamon-flavored sauce glazes these birds-on-a-spit.

Makes 4 servings.

¹/₂ cup (1 stick) butter or margarine
4 teaspoons ground cinnamon
1 teaspoon curry powder
¹/₄ teaspoon garlic powder
2 whole broiler-fryers (about 2 pounds each)
1 large onion, sliced
¹/₄ cup honey

1. Melt butter or margarine in a small saucepan; stir in 3 teaspoons of the cinnamon and curry and garlic powders; heat until bubbly.
2. Wash chickens inside and out; remove packets of giblets, if any, and set aside to simmer for broth to use in soup or gravy. Pat chickens dry.
3. Sprinkle ¹/₂ teaspoon of the remaining cinnamon and place half of the onion slices inside each chicken. Skewer neck skin to body; secure body cavity closed and tie legs tightly to tail.
4. Place chickens on spit; brush with part of the cinnamon butter. Set spit in position over hot coals; start rotisserie.
5. Roast 1 hour, brushing several times with more cinnamon butter.
6. Stir honey into remaining cinnamon butter in pan; brush over chickens. Roast 15 minutes longer, or until tender and richly glazed.
7. Remove to a cutting board; take out spit. Cut chickens into quarters with kitchen scissors.

CHICKEN ASADO

A touch of wine gives flavor to over-the-coals chicken.

Makes 4 servings.

2 cups olive oil
2 cups vinegar
1 cup dry white wine
1 tablespoon snipped parsley
1 tablespoon salt
2 teaspoons oregano
1 teaspoon red pepper flakes
1 teaspoon thyme

1 clove garlic, minced
2 broiler-fryers (about 2 pounds each),
   split in half

1. Combine all ingredients except chicken; mix well in saucepan; heat to boiling.
2. Coat chicken halves with sauce, place on grill over hot coals.
3. Baste frequently with hot sauce and turn several times so that chicken cooks evenly on both sides. Cook until fork-tender (about 1¼ hours).
4. Serve hot and pass any extra sauce.

GRILLED CINNAMON-HONEY CHICKEN

You can grill it outdoors, but this is no woodman's dish — note the rather elegant marinade.
Makes 8 servings.

2 broiler-fryers (2 to 2½ pounds each),
   quartered
1 cup dry sherry
²/₃ cup honey
4 teaspoons cinnamon
2 teaspoons curry powder
2 teaspoons garlic salt

1. Place chicken quarters in a shallow baking pan. Combine ingredients for marinade and blend well; pour over chicken.

2. Cover and allow to stand at room temperature 2 to 3 hours, or refrigerate 8 hours or overnight; drain off marinade, reserving for basting sauce.
3. Place chicken on grill, skin side up, over hot coals. Turn quarters about every 10 minutes, basting with reserved marinade to keep chicken juicy.
4. Cook slowly 1¼ to 1½ hours. Chicken is ready to serve when drumstick twists out of thigh joint readily, and thickest portions are fork-tender. (Note: Chicken will be dark brown when grilled, due to the marinade.)

CHICKEN ON A SPIT

Currant jelly glazes this chicken as it twirls on the rotisserie.

Makes 4 to 6 servings.

2 cups ready-mix bread stuffing
½ cup (1 stick) butter or margarine, melted
²/₃ cup water
1 roasting chicken (about 4 pounds)
½ cup currant jelly, melted

1. Prepare stuffing mix with ⅓ cup of the melted butter or margarine and water, fol-

lowing label directions on package.
2. Wash chicken, then dry. Stuff neck and body cavities lightly; skewer neck skin to body; secure body cavity closed and tie legs tightly to tail.
3. Place chicken on spit; brush with remaining butter or margarine. Set spit in position over hot coals; start spit turning.
4. Roast 1 hour; brush with melted jelly. Continue roasting, brushing often with more jelly, 15 minutes longer, or until chicken is tender and richly glazed.

GRILLED CHICKEN BREASTS SUPREME

This exotic chicken from the Far East is especially good with Tibetan rice and a tangy fruit sauce.

Makes 4 servings.

4 whole chicken breasts
$^{1}/_{2}$ cup flour
1 teaspoon salt
$^{1}/_{8}$ teaspoon pepper
$^{1}/_{8}$ teaspoon nutmeg
1 egg
1 tablespoon water
1 cup finely ground cashew nuts
  ($^{1}/_{2}$ pound)
4 green onions, chopped
2 tablespoons chopped parsley
4 tablespoons ($^{1}/_{2}$ stick) butter or
  margarine, melted
Tibetan Rice
3 cups Piquant Fruit Sauce

1. Wash and dry chicken; cut out any small rib bones and breastbones so breasts will lie flat, butterfly style. Shake in mixture of flour, salt, pepper, and nutmeg in paper bag to coat well.
2. Beat egg with water in pie plate; place ground cashew nuts in second pie plate. Dip chicken in egg mixture, then in nuts.
3. Place each breast, skin side up, on a 12-inch square of heavy foil. Sprinkle with green onions and parsley; drizzle melted butter or margarine over.
4. Wrap foil around chicken and seal tightly with a drugstore fold; place on grill above hot coals. Grill, turning often, 1 hour, or until chicken is tender.
5. Split foil envelopes open; place each breast on a bed of Tibetan Rice; serve with Piquant Fruit Sauce.

TIBETAN RICE

Makes 4 servings.

$^{3}/_{4}$ cup raw rice
2 tablespoons salad oil
$^{1}/_{2}$ teaspoon turmeric
$^{1}/_{2}$ teaspoon curry powder
$^{1}/_{2}$ teaspoon salt
$^{1}/_{4}$ cup seedless raisins
Water
1 can condensed chicken consomme
  OR 2 chicken bouillon cubes

1. Stir rice into salad oil in top of medium-size double boiler; heat over direct heat, stirring constantly, until rice is well-coated.
2. Blend in turmeric, curry powder, and salt; stir in raisins. Add enough water to consomme to make 1½ cups (or use bouillon cubes dissolved in 1½ cups boiling water); stir into rice mixture.
3. Cover; cook over simmering water 1 hour, or until rice is fluffed and tender and liquid is absorbed.

PIQUANT FRUIT SAUCE

Makes about 3 cups.

2 tablespoons brown sugar
1 teaspoon cornstarch
1 teaspoon salt
1 can (1 pound, 4 ounces) pineapple
  chunks
$^{1}/_{2}$ cup orange juice
1 tablespoon lemon juice
$^{1}/_{4}$ cup water
1 can (about 11 ounces) mandarin orange
  sections, drained

1. Blend brown sugar, cornstarch, and salt in medium-size saucepan; stir in pineapple and syrup, orange and lemon juices, and water.
2. Cook, stirring constantly, until sauce thickens slightly and boils 3 minutes. Stir in mandarin orange sections; heat just to boiling.

STUFFED WHIRLYBIRD

Rotisserie chicken with a fruity or spicy stuffing.

Makes 4 servings.

1 roasting chicken (about 4 pounds)
Fruit Stuffing OR packaged Spanish Rice
  Stuffing
Butter or margarine (1 to 2 tablespoons)
Salt
Pepper
Ginger-Honey Glaze

1. Wash and dry chicken.
2. Stuff breast and body cavities with either Fruit Stuffing (from recipe at right) or Spanish Rice Stuffing (follow label directions).
3. Secure body and neck cavities tightly closed; tie legs and wings tightly to body. Rub bird with softened butter or margarine and sprinkle with salt and pepper.
4. Place on rotisserie spit and roast 1 hour, then begin basting with Ginger-Honey Glaze. Continue roasting, basting often, 30 to 45 minutes longer, or until chicken is richly browned and tender.

GINGER-HONEY GLAZE: Combine ½ cup soy sauce, 6 tablespoons honey, and 2 teaspoons ground ginger in small saucepan. Heat, stirring constantly, just to boiling. Makes about ¾ cup, or enough for two roasting chickens.

FRUIT STUFFING

Makes 7 cups.

1 can (1 pound) sliced apples
Water
¹/₂ cup (1 stick) butter or margarine
1 package (2 cups) ready-mix bread
  stuffing
1 cup chopped peanuts
¹/₂ cup seedless raisins

1. Drain sliced apples; add water to apple liquid to make 1 cup; heat to boiling in large saucepan.
2. Stir in butter or margarine until melted; add ready-mix bread stuffing, sliced apples, peanuts, and raisins, tossing lightly to mix.
3. Stuff chicken. Wrap any remaining stuffing in foil; cook on grill about 1 hour, while chicken roasts.

PERFECT CHICKEN BARBECUE

A beginner's guide to perfect grilled chicken.

Makes 8 servings.

4 broiler-fryers (about 2 pounds each),
  halved
4 teaspoons monosodium glutamate
2 teaspoons salt
2 teaspoons pepper
Salad oil

1. Sprinkle each chicken half with ½ teaspoon monosodium glutamate, ¼ teaspoon salt, ¼ teaspoon pepper. Brush lightly with oil.
2. Place chicken, skin side up, on grate set 3 to 6 inches from heat.
3. Cook slowly, turning occasionally and basting lightly with more oil if meat seems to be drying out. Allow 45 minutes to 1¼ hours cooking time. To test for doneness, leg should twist easily out of thigh joint, and meat should be fork-tender.

BROILED CHICKEN

Broiled chicken dishes tend to be uncomplicated and offer the advantage of relatively quick cooking — they are ready in 40 minutes or so. Keep an eye on your broiling chicken and baste or turn it as the recipe directs, so it won't dry out. When a broiled chicken is done, it will be fork-tender, and a drumstick will move easily at the joint.

LEMON BROILED CHICKEN

Light and appetizing chicken that makes few demands on the budget, the digestion, or the cook.

Makes 4 servings.

1 broiler-fryer (3 pounds), cut in quarters
1 teaspoon monosodium glutamate
Salt
Pepper
Paprika
Juice of ¹/₂ lemon
2 teaspoons salad oil
1 teaspoon tarragon

1. Sprinkle chicken with monosodium glutamate, salt, pepper, and paprika.
2. Line broiler pan with aluminum foil. Turn temperature control to moderate (350°) and broil 3 to 4 inches from heat, or set control for "broil" and place broiler pan 7 to 8 inches from heat.

3. Place chicken, skin side down, on pan. Combine lemon juice, salad oil, and tarragon; brush ½ mixture over chicken.
4. Broil 30 minutes, brushing occasionally with pan drippings. Turn chicken and brush with remaining lemon-herb mixture. Broil 15 to 30 minutes longer, brushing occasionally. Chicken is done when pieces are fork-tender.

BROILED CHICKEN BING

Elegant sweet-sour cherry sauce dresses up crisply broiled chicken.

Makes 6 servings.

**3 broiler-fryers (about 2 pounds each),
  split**
2 cups Dark Cherry Sauce

1. Wash chickens; pat dry. Place, skin side down, on rack in broiler pan.
2. Broil, turning every 10 minutes, until chickens are tender and brown — about 40 minutes. Remove to heated serving platter.
3. Spoon hot Dark Cherry Sauce over all and serve immediately.

DARK CHERRY SAUCE

Makes about 2 cups.

1 can (1 pound) pitted dark sweet cherries
2 tablespoons cornstarch
1 tablespoon prepared mustard
1 tablespoon molasses
Few drops red-pepper seasoning
Dash of salt
3 tablespoons lemon juice

1. Drain syrup from cherries into a 2-cup measure; add water to make 1½ cups. (Save cherries for Step 3.)
2. Blend a few tablespoons syrup into cornstarch until smooth in a small saucepan; stir in remaining syrup, mustard, molasses, red-pepper seasoning, and salt. Cook over low heat, stirring constantly, until mixture thickens and boils 3 minutes.
3. Stir in cherries and lemon juice; heat slowly just until bubbly. Serve hot.

BROILED CHICKEN WITH CREAM SAUCE

Broiled chicken breasts are served on crisp bacon and blanketed with creamy sauce.

Makes 6 servings.

**3 large whole chicken breasts, split
  (about 2 pounds)**
**¼ cup (½ stick) butter or margarine,
  melted**
1 can (about 11 ounces) chicken gravy
¼ cup light or table cream
1 teaspoon lemon juice
2 or 3 drops red-pepper seasoning
**12 slices Canadian-style bacon (about
  ½ pound)**

1. Remove skin from chicken and cut away meat from bones in one piece. (Use a sharp thin-bladed knife, cutting close to bones, and meat will pull away easily; simmer bones in water for a broth for another day, if you wish.)
2. Place chicken, rounded side down, on greased broiler rack; brush with half the melted butter or margarine; broil about 10 minutes; turn; brush again with remaining butter or margarine; broil 10 to 12 minutes longer, or until golden-brown and tender when pierced with a fork.
3. While chicken cooks, combine chicken gravy, cream, lemon juice, and red-pepper seasoning in small saucepan; heat, stirring often, just to boiling.
4. Arrange bacon slices in single layer in shallow pan; 2 to 3 minutes before chicken is done, slide pan into hot oven (from broiling chicken) to cook bacon and crisp any fat edges.
5. Put 2 slices bacon on each dinner plate; top with half a chicken breast; spoon about ¼ cup heated sauce over.

BROILED CHICKEN FLAMBE

Here's one way to dress up simple broiled chicken: baste it with a fragrant sauce, serve it flaming.

Makes 4 servings.

1 broiler-fryer (3 pounds), quartered
6 tablespoons melted butter or margarine
1/2 teaspoon rosemary
1/2 teaspoon sweet basil
1/4 teaspoon garlic powder
1/4 teaspoon salt
1/4 teaspoon pepper
Parsley or celery leaves for garnish
Dash of paprika
1/4 cup rum

1. Place chicken quarters in broiler and baste with mixture of butter and seasonings. Broil, basting several times, about 40 minutes or until done. Remove to large, deep heated platter.
2. Dust parsley or celery leaves with paprika and arrange around chicken.
3. Warm rum slightly, ignite it, pour instantly over chicken on platter and serve flaming.

KEY LIME CHICKEN BROIL

A zesty splash of lime and tarragon seasons tender broiled chicken.

Makes 6 servings.

3 broiler-fryers (about 2 pounds each), split
1/2 cup lime juice
1/2 cup vegetable oil
1 tablespoon grated onion
2 teaspoons tarragon, crushed
1 teaspoon seasoned salt
1/4 teaspoon seasoned pepper

1. Wash chickens; pat dry. Place, skin side down, on rack in broiler pan.
2. Mix lime juice, vegetable oil, onion, tarragon, and seasoned salt and pepper in a small bowl. Brush generously over chickens.
3. Broil, turning every 10 minutes and brushing with more lime mixture, 40 minutes or until chickens are tender and richly browned. Remove to a heated large serving platter.

APPLE-WINE BROILER CHICKEN

True apple flavor comes through in this easygoing chicken.

Makes 8 servings.

2 broiler-fryers (2 1/2 to 3 pounds), split in half
1/2 cup (8 tablespoons) melted butter or margarine
2 teaspoons salt
2 tablespoons apple jelly
1/4 cup white wine

1. Brush chicken halves thoroughly with butter or margarine. Sprinkle with salt.
2. Mash apple jelly with a fork, then add wine gradually. Brush this mixture on both sides of chicken halves.
3. Place chicken, skin side down, in broiler pan (without rack). Broil 6 to 9 inches from the heat for 30 minutes. Then turn skin side up and continue broiling until chicken is evenly browned and cooked, about 20 minutes longer.
4. Cut each half into quarters for serving.

CHICKEN STEWS

A chicken-in-the-pot, with seasonings and vegetables, gives you a whole hearty meal in one dish. Because stews cook a long while, you can often use a large, economical, and comparatively old chicken — as many of these recipes indicate. In the simmering, even a big bird turns to falling-apart tenderness. Many stews, or fricassees as they are sometimes called, have dumplings, cooked in the liquid with the meat. An extra-hearty stew made up in a large batch is known, in affectionate slang, as a "burgoo." A recipe for such a stew appears in the section on CHICKEN FOR A CROWD. A few fine stews containing chicken legs may be found in the section, DRUMSTICKS.

PIMIENTO CHICKEN STEW

A hearty meal topped with peppy pimiento biscuits.

Makes 8 servings.

1 stewing chicken (4 to 5 pounds), cut in serving-size pieces
1/2 cup flour
1 envelope herb salad dressing mix
1 large onion, chopped (1 cup)
2 cans (about 1 pound each) tomatoes
2 cups water
1 teaspoon sugar
2 cups diced celery
2 cups fresh lima beans OR 1 can (about 1 pound) lima beans and liquid (cut water to 1 1/2 cups)
1 1/2 cups fresh corn kernels or 1 can (12 or 16 ounces) whole-kernel corn
1 can (4 ounces) pimientos
1/4 cup chopped parsley
Pimiento Biscuits

1. Remove all fat from chicken, and skin from breasts, thighs, and drumsticks; melt fat in large heavy kettle or Dutch oven.
2. Shake chicken with flour and salad-dressing mix in paper bag to coat evenly; brown, a few pieces at a time, in fat in kettle. Remove chicken and set aside.
3. Sauté onion until soft in same kettle; stir in tomatoes, water, and sugar; add celery, lima beans, corn, and chicken.
4. Cover; simmer 1 hour, or until chicken is tender; let stand 5 to 10 minutes; skim off any excess fat.
5. Save 1 pimiento for Pimiento Biscuits; dice remaining; stir into stew with parsley; serve with Pimiento Biscuits.

PIMIENTO BISCUITS

Bake at 400° for 10 minutes.
Makes 12 biscuits.

1 3/4 cups biscuit mix
1/2 cup yellow cornmeal
2 tablespoons melted butter or margarine
1 pimiento, chopped
2/3 cup milk

1. Mix biscuit mix, cornmeal, melted butter or margarine, and pimiento with a fork in a medium-size bowl; stir in milk just until no dry mix appears; spoon in 12 mounds onto ungreased cooky sheet.
2. Bake in hot oven (400°) 10 minutes, or until golden.

CHICKEN QUEBEC

Serve this spoon-up main dish in soup plates to enjoy with thick slices of crusty French bread.

Simmer 2 hours.

Makes 6 servings.

1 stewing chicken (about 5 pounds), cut into serving-size pieces
6 slices Canadian-style bacon
1 medium-size onion, chopped (¹/₂ cup)
1 teaspoon salt
3 or 4 peppercorns
6 cups water
1 package (8 ounces) elbow macaroni
1 tablespoon parsley flakes

1. Trim fat from chicken; melt fat in large heavy kettle or Dutch oven. Brown chicken, a few serving pieces at a time; drain on paper toweling.

2. Fry bacon lightly in same kettle; remove and set aside; pour off all fat. Return browned chicken and bacon to kettle; add onion, salt, peppercorns, and water.

3. Cover tightly; heat to boiling, then simmer 2 hours, or until chicken is tender. (If much fat has cooked out, remove kettle from heat; let stand 5 to 10 minutes; then skim off fat.)

4. Reheat to boiling; stir in macaroni and parsley flakes. (Add 1 cup water, if needed.) Cook, uncovered, stirring occasionally, 15 to 20 minutes, or until macaroni is tender. Taste and add salt, if needed.

Note: If little new potatoes are in season, use in place of macaroni. Leave jackets on and cook in stew, covered, until tender.

CHICKEN GUMBO

The fabulous Creole cuisine of Louisiana combines many influences, including French, Spanish, American Indian, and African.

Makes 8 servings.

1 stewing chicken (4 to 5 pounds), cut in serving-size pieces
1 tablespoon salt
¹/₂ teaspoon pepper
1 stick (¹/₂ cup) butter or margarine
6 tablespoons flour
2 medium-size onions, chopped (1 cup)
1 clove garlic, crushed
4 to 5 quarts water
¹/₂ pound uncooked shrimp, shelled and deveined
2 cups diced okra
¹/₂ cup chopped parsley
¹/₂ cup diced celery
¹/₂ cup chopped scallions
¹/₄ teaspoon thyme

1. Season chicken with salt and pepper. Heat butter or margarine in a large skillet and fry chicken until golden brown. Remove chicken to a heavy kettle or Dutch oven.

2. Add flour to fat in skillet and cook until lightly brown. Add onion and garlic clove; simmer until onion is transparent.

3. Pour contents of skillet into kettle with chicken; pour in 1 quart of the water slowly; cover and simmer 1 hour or until chicken is almost tender.

4. Add shrimp, okra, and 3 or 4 quarts water; simmer 20 minutes longer.

5. Add parsley, celery, scallions, and thyme, and simmer 15 minutes longer.

6. Ladle over cooked rice on 8 plates.

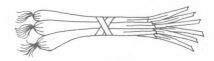

ALL-IN-ONE CHICKEN DINNER

An economical way to feed a family well with only a few cups of cooked chicken on hand.

Makes 6 servings.

2 cups chicken stock, broth, or bouillon
12 small white onions (¹/₂ pound)
6 medium-size carrots, cut in 2-inch pieces
1 package frozen lima beans
¹/₂ cup chicken fat, butter, or margarine
¹/₂ cup flour
1 teaspoon thyme
1 teaspoon salt
¹/₈ teaspoon pepper
1 teaspoon Worcestershire sauce
2 cups milk
3 cups cooked chicken (boiled, broiled, or roasted), cut into large pieces
Cranberry Biscuits

1. Put chicken stock in a kettle and bring to boiling; add onions, carrots, and lima beans; reheat to boiling, cook 15 minutes, or until vegetables are tender.
2. Heat chicken fat, butter, or margarine in large saucepan while vegetables cook; remove from heat.
3. Blend in flour, thyme, salt, pepper, and Worcestershire sauce.
4. Drain vegetables, saving stock; save vegetables for Step 6; blend stock into flour mixture; stir in milk.
5. Cook over low heat, stirring constantly,

until gravy thickens and boils 1 minute; remove from heat.
6. Stir in chicken and cooked vegetables; set aside while you make Cranberry Biscuits.
7. Reheat chicken mixture over low heat, stirring often to avoid scorching, while biscuits bake.
8. Pour hot chicken mixture into heated serving dish as soon as biscuits are done; top with biscuits; serve at once.

CRANBERRY BISCUITS

Bake at 450° for 10 to 15 minutes.
Makes 6 large biscuits.

2 cups biscuit mix
²/₃ cup milk
About 6 tablespoons canned whole-cranberry sauce

1. Blend biscuit mix and milk with fork in medium-size bowl just until dry ingredients are dampened.
2. Drop in 6 mounds onto buttered cooky sheet; make a depression on top of each mound of dough with back of teaspoon.
3. Bake in hot oven (450°) 10 to 15 minutes, or until biscuits are golden-brown.
4. Fill depressions in biscuits with cranberry sauce just before serving.

CHICKEN DUMPLING POTPIE

A hearty meal-in-one: chicken, dumplings, green peas, potatoes cooked in broth.

Makes 4 servings.

1 broiler-fryer (about 2¹/₂ pounds), cut up
1 large onion, sliced
2 teaspoons salt
¹/₂ teaspoon ground ginger
¹/₂ teaspoon marjoram
4 cups water
3 medium-size potatoes, pared, quartered
Dumpling Squares
2 tablespoons butter or margarine
1 can (about 1 pound) green peas
2 tablespoons flour

1. Combine chicken with onion, salt, ginger, marjoram, and water in a Dutch oven; cover.
2. Simmer 1 hour, or until tender; remove chicken; set aside for Step 4.
3. Strain broth and return to pan. Add potatoes; heat to boiling, then add Dumpling Squares, a few at a time, stirring with a fork to keep them from sticking together. Cover tightly; cook 20 minutes.
4. While potatoes and dumplings cook, brown chicken lightly in butter or margarine in a large frying pan. Heat peas in their liquid to boiling in a small saucepan.
5. Lift potatoes and Dumpling Squares from broth and place in a heated shallow dish; pile browned chicken on top; sprinkle with chopped parsley, if you wish. Keep hot while making gravy from potato-dumpling broth.
6. Blend flour into drippings in frying pan; stir in chicken broth, adding water, if needed, to make 2 cups. Cook, stirring constantly, until gravy thickens and boils 1 minute. Serve separately.

DUMPLING SQUARES: Combine 1 cup sifted flour, ¼ teaspoon baking powder, and ¼ teaspoon salt in a medium-size bowl. Beat 1 egg with 1 tablespoon milk and 1 tablespoon melted butter or margarine in a 1-cup measure; stir into flour mixture until evenly moist. Turn out onto a lightly floured pastry cloth or board; knead a few times to make a smooth dough. Roll out to a square, 8x8; cut into 16 2-inch squares with knife or pastry wheel. Cover until ready to cook.

CHICKEN CREOLE

Tomato-onion-green-pepper combination distinctively flavors a Louisiana classic.

Makes 4 to 6 servings.

1 broiler-fryer (about 3 pounds), cut in serving-size pieces
1 teaspoon monosodium glutamate
1¹/₂ teaspoons salt
¹/₂ teaspoon paprika
3 tablespoons salad oil
¹/₄ cup water
1 medium onion, sliced
1 medium green pepper, seeded, sliced
¹/₂ cup diced celery
1 can (1 pound) tomatoes
1 teaspoon dried thyme
2 tablespoons chopped parsley

1. Sprinkle chicken pieces with monosodium glutamate, ½ teaspoon of the salt, and paprika.
2. Place chicken pieces, skin side down, in heated oil in skillet. Brown on both sides; remove from skillet.
3. Add water, scraping brown particles from bottom of pan. Add onion, green pepper, and celery; cover; cook 5 minutes.
4. Add remaining teaspoon salt, chicken pieces, tomatoes, and tarragon. Heat to boiling. Cover; reduce heat and simmer 40 minutes.
5. Turn into serving dish; sprinkle with parsley. Serve over hot cooked rice.

CHICKEN 'N' EGGS GOURMET

Most of the preparation for this dish can be done ahead of time.

Makes 6 to 7 servings.

1 stewing chicken (4 to 6 pounds), cut up
4 cups water
8 medium-size onions, chopped (4 cups)
¼ cup chicken fat
2 cups hot chicken broth
3 teaspoons salt
2 teaspoons chili powder
½ teaspoon pepper
¼ cup lemon juice
¼ cup red wine
1 teaspoon crushed tarragon
½ teaspoon ground ginger
6 hard-cooked eggs, whole, shelled

1. Simmer chicken, including giblets and neck, in water until thickest pieces are fork-tender, about 2½ hours. Remove chicken; cool; spoon off fat from broth and reserve. This much can be done the day or morning before.
2. About 40 minutes before mealtime, measure ¼ cup fat and 2 cups broth (reserve remaining fat and broth for future cooking).
3. Cook onion in the ¼ cup chicken fat in skillet until tender but not brown. Add 1 cup of the broth, salt, chili powder, and pepper. Simmer, uncovered, for 5 minutes.
4. Add lemon juice, wine, tarragon, and ginger and the second cup of broth. Place chicken and eggs in the sauce. Cover and simmer about 30 minutes or until chicken and eggs have absorbed some of the color from the sauce. Serve hot.

BROWN CHICKEN FRICASSEE

Chicken browned with onions and topped off with cornmeal dumplings should please all grown men and little boys.

Makes 6 servings.

1 stewing chicken (about 5 pounds), cut up
¼ cup flour
2 teaspoons salt
1 teaspoon poultry seasoning
¼ teaspoon pepper
3 tablespoons salad oil
2 medium-size onions, sliced and
  separated into rings
1 bay leaf
4 cups water
Cornmeal Dumplings

1. Wash chicken; drain. Shake pieces, a few at a time, in mixture of flour, salt, poultry seasoning, and pepper in a paper bag to coat well.
2. Brown slowly in salad oil in a large heavy frying pan; remove. Add onion rings, sauté until they are soft.
3. Return chicken to pan; add bay leaf and water; cover. Simmer 1½ hours or until chicken is tender.
4. Prepare Cornmeal Dumplings. Heat chicken until boiling rapidly; drop dough into 12 small mounds on top; cover.
5. Cook, covered, 20 minutes. (No peeking, or the dumplings won't puff properly.)
6. Remove chicken and dumplings to a heated serving platter; remove bay leaf; serve gravy in a separate bowl.

CORNMEAL DUMPLINGS: Sift 1½ cups sifted flour, ¼ cup yellow cornmeal, 3 teaspoons baking powder, and 1 teaspoon salt into a medium-size bowl. Cut in 2 tablespoons shortening with a pastry blender until mixture is crumbly. Stir in 1 cup milk just until flour mixture is moistened. (Dough will be soft.)

POT-ROASTED CHICKEN WITH CREAM GRAVY

A French way of simmering a large chicken to savory tenderness.

Makes 4 to 6 servings.

4 tablespoons (¹/₂ stick) butter or margarine
1 stewing chicken (4 to 5 pounds)
2 teaspoons leaf thyme
1 can condensed beef broth
3 tablespoons flour
1 small can evaporated milk (²/₃ cup)

1. Melt butter or margarine in heavy kettle or Dutch oven; brush part on inside of chicken, then sprinkle chicken with 1 teaspoon thyme. Brown chicken lightly on all sides in remaining butter or margarine.
2. Turn chicken, breast side up; pour beef broth over; sprinkle with remaining 1 teaspoon thyme; cover tightly.
3. Simmer, basting a few times with pan juices, 1½ hours, or until tender. Remove to heated serving platter; keep hot while making gravy.
4. Pour broth from kettle into 4-cup measure. Let fat rise to top, then skim off. Add water to broth, if needed, to make 2½ cups.
5. Return 2 tablespoons fat to kettle; blend in flour; stir in broth. Cook, stirring constantly, until gravy thickens and boils 1 minute. Blend in evaporated milk; heat just to boiling.
6. Serve chicken with buttered noodles and spoon gravy over all.

DAPPLED DUMPLING FRICASSEE

Kettle chicken cooked tender, served with gravy and topped with parsley-sprigged dumplings.

Makes 6 servings.

1 stewing chicken (about 5 pounds), cut up
4 cups plus ¹/₂ cup cold water
1 large onion, sliced
1 cup chopped celery and leaves
1 medium-size carrot, scraped and sliced
2 teaspoons salt
¹/₄ teaspoon pepper
6 tablespoons flour
Dappled Dumplings

1. Combine chicken, 4 cups water, onion, celery and leaves, carrot, salt, and pepper in large kettle or Dutch oven with tight-fitting cover. Cover; heat to boiling, then simmer 1½ to 2 hours, or until chicken is tender.
2. Remove from broth; cool slightly; slip off skin, if you wish. Strain and measure broth; add water, if needed, to make 5 cups. Press vegetables through strainer into broth in kettle; heat to boiling.
3. Stir ½ cup cold water into flour in cup to make a smooth paste; stir into hot broth. Cook, stirring constantly, until gravy thickens and boils 1 minute. Season with salt and pepper to taste, if needed.
4. Return chicken to gravy in kettle; heat slowly to boiling while stirring up Dappled Dumplings.
5. Drop dough in 12 mounds on top of steaming chicken. Cook, covered, 20 minutes. (No peeking, or the dumplings won't puff properly.)
6. Arrange chicken and dumplings on a heated serving platter; pass gravy in separate bowl.

DAPPLED DUMPLINGS: Sift 2 cups sifted flour, 3 teaspoons baking powder, and 1 teaspoon salt into medium-size bowl. Cut in 2 tablespoons shortening with pastry blender until mixture is crumbly. Stir in ¼ cup chopped parsley and 1 cup milk just until flour is moistened. (Dough will be soft.)

CHICKEN PIES

The word "pie" has a built-in magic, especially for youngsters, and in fact for almost everyone who doesn't keep an apprehensive eye on the scales. Chicken pie is somewhat a labor of love, but well worth it (and sometimes you can cut corners with a pastry mix). Here are three savory pies with crust, one with biscuit topping, and one big puffy chicken popover.

COUNTRY CHICKEN PIE

A medley of flavors — chicken, ham, pimiento, onion — make this a dinner you'll want to serve often.

Bake at 400° for 40 minutes.
Makes 6 to 8 servings.

1 broiler-fryer (about 3¹/₂ pounds), cut up
Few celery tops
2¹/₂ teaspoons salt
1 tablespoon instant minced onion
2¹/₂ cups water
¹/₂ cup (1 stick) butter or margarine
¹/₂ cup flour
¹/₈ teaspoon pepper
Dash of mace
1 can (about 1 pound) whole boiled onions, drained
2 cups cubed cooked ham
1 can (4 ounces) pimientos, drained and diced
¹/₂ package piecrust mix

1. Combine chicken, celery tops, 2 teaspoons of the salt, minced onion, and water in a kettle; heat to boiling; cover. Simmer 30 minutes, or until chicken is tender.
2. Remove from broth; cool until easy to handle. Strain broth into a 4-cup measure; add water, if needed, to make 2½ cups. Pull skin from chicken and take meat from bones; dice meat.
3. Melt butter or margarine in a large saucepan; blend in flour, remaining ½ teaspoon salt, pepper, and mace. Cook, stirring constantly, just until bubbly. Stir in the 2½ cups chicken broth; continue cooking and stirring until sauce thickens and boils 1 minute; remove from heat.
4. Stir in onions, diced chicken, ham, and pimientos; spoon into a shallow 10-cup baking dish. Keep hot in oven while mixing pastry.
5. Prepare piecrust mix, following label directions, or make pastry from your own single-crust recipe. Roll out on a lightly floured pastry cloth or board to a rectangle or round 1 inch larger than baking dish; cut several slits in center to let steam escape. Place over chicken mixture in baking dish; trim overhang to ½ inch; turn edge under, flush with rim; flute edge all around.
6. Bake in hot oven (400°) 40 minutes, or until pastry is golden.

CRISSCROSS CHICKEN PIE

This would be grandmother's idea of a stick-to-the-ribs dinner.

Bake at 400° for 20 minutes, then at 350° for 25 minutes.

Makes 6 servings.

1 broiler-fryer (3 pounds), cut up
3 cups water
Handful of celery tops
2 teaspoons salt
6 peppercorns
Curry Cream Sauce
1 package (10 ounces) frozen peas, cooked and drained
1 pimiento, chopped
2 cups sifted flour
$1/_3$ cup shortening
$2/_3$ cup milk

1. Simmer chicken with water, celery tops, 1 teaspoon salt, and peppercorns in kettle 1 hour, or until tender. Remove from broth and let cool until easy to handle.

2. Strain broth into 4-cup measure; add water, if needed, to make 3 cups. Make Curry Cream Sauce.

3. Slip skin from chicken, then remove meat from bones. (It comes off easily while still warm.) Cut into bite-size pieces; toss with peas, pimiento, and 2 cups of Curry Cream Sauce in medium-size bowl. Set aside for Step 5. (Save remaining sauce to reheat and serve over pie.)

4. Sift flour and 1 teaspoon salt into medium-size bowl; cut in shortening with pastry blender until mixture is crumbly; stir in milk with a fork just until dough holds together.

5. Turn out onto lightly floured pastry cloth or board; knead lightly 5 or 6 times. Roll out ⅔ of dough to a rectangle, 16x12; fit into a baking dish, 10x6x2. Spoon filling into shell.

6. Roll out remaining pastry to a rectangle about 14x7; cut into 9 long strips, each about ¾ inch wide, with knife or pastry wheel. Lay 5 strips lengthwise over filling. Halve remaining 4 strips; weave across long strips to make a crisscross top. Trim overhang to 1 inch; fold under; flute.

7. Bake in hot oven (400°) 20 minutes; reduce heat to moderate (350°). Bake 25 minutes longer, or until golden. Cut into 6 servings. Serve with remaining hot Curry Cream Sauce.

CURRY CREAM SAUCE: Melt 6 tablespoons (¾ stick) butter or margarine over low heat in medium-size saucepan. Stir in 6 tablespoons flour, 1 teaspoon salt, 1 teaspoon curry powder, and ⅛ teaspoon pepper. Cook, stirring all the time, just until mixture bubbles. Stir in 3 cups chicken broth slowly; continue cooking and stirring until sauce thickens and boils 1 minute. Stir in 1 tall can evaporated milk. Makes about 4½ cups.

JUMBO CHICKEN POPOVER

This turns out to be an oversize puffy pop-over containing browned chicken parts.

Bake at 350° for 1 hour.

Makes 4 servings.

1 broiler-fryer (about 3 pounds)
4 tablespoons plus 1½ cups flour
2 teaspoons salt
1 teaspoon paprika
¼ teaspoon pepper
Fat for frying
1½ teaspoons baking powder
4 eggs
1½ cups milk
3 tablespoons melted butter or margarine
Cream Gravy

1. Cut chicken into 8 pieces — 2 breasts, 2 wings, 2 thighs, 2 drumsticks. Cut away back and any small bones from breasts; simmer bones with neck and giblets in 1 cup water in small saucepan. Strain to make broth for Cream Gravy (for recipe, turn to section on GRAVIES).

2. Shake chicken pieces with 4 table-spoons flour, 1 teaspoon salt, paprika, and pepper in paper bag to coat lightly.

3. Brown, a few at a time, in hot fat in heavy frying pan; drain on paper towel.

4. Sift 1½ cups flour, baking powder, and 1 teaspoon salt into medium bowl.

5. Beat eggs slightly in second medium-size bowl; blend in milk and melted butter or margarine. Stir slowly into dry ingredients; then beat with rotary beater just until smooth.

6. Pour batter into buttered shallow 8-cup baking dish; arrange browned chicken pieces in batter.

7. Bake in moderate oven (350°) 1 hour, or until puffed and golden brown. (Pop-over around chicken bakes like a big puff, so keep oven door closed for full hour.)

8. Serve at once with Cream Gravy.

DEEP-DISH CHICKEN PIE

Not for dieters but guaranteed to fill up a famished family.

Bake at 425° for 30 minutes.

Makes 6 servings.

6 medium-size potatoes, pared, quartered
6 medium-size carrots, scraped and
  quartered
1 small onion, chopped (¼ cup)
¼ cup chopped green pepper
2 tablespoons butter or margarine
1 can condensed cream of chicken soup
3 cups chunks of cooked chicken (boiled,
  roasted, or broiled)
Biscuit Wedge Topping

1. Cook potatoes and carrots in boiling salted water in large saucepan 15 to 20 minutes, or until tender; drain, saving 1 cup of liquid for next step.

2. While vegetables cook, sauté onion and green pepper in butter or margarine until soft in saucepan; stir in chicken soup and 1 cup saved liquid.

3. Spoon vegetables and chicken into 8-cup casserole; pour sauce over.

4. Bake in hot oven (425°) 15 minutes while making Biscuit Wedge Topping; arrange biscuits on top of hot mixture; bake 15 minutes longer, or until biscuits are golden.

BISCUIT WEDGE TOPPING: Sift 1½ cups sifted flour, 2 teaspoons baking powder, and ½ teaspoon salt into medium-size bowl; cut in ¼ cup (½ stick) butter or margarine; add ½ cup milk all at once; stir just until blended. Turn dough out onto lightly floured pastry cloth or board; knead lightly ½ minute; roll out to a 7-inch round; cut into 6 wedges; brush tops lightly with milk; sprinkle with ¼ teaspoon poppy seeds.

CHICKEN A LA KING PIE

A very special chicken pie: white meat in a luscious cream sauce, baked under a pastry crust.

Bake at 425° for 15 minutes.

Makes 6 to 8 servings.

3 chicken breasts (about 12 ounces each)
Few celery tops
1 small onion, chopped (¹/₄ cup)
6 peppercorns
1 teaspoon salt
2 envelopes instant chicken broth
**   or 2 chicken bouillon cubes**
1 cup water
1 cup light or table cream
1 can or jar (2 ounces) sliced pimientos,
**   drained**
1 cup diced celery
1 small green pepper, halved, seeded,
**   and diced (¹/₂ cup)**
4 tablespoons (¹/₂ stick) butter or margarine
¹/₂ cup flour
1 can (3 or 4 ounces) whole mushrooms
¹/₂ cup dry sherry
¹/₂ package piecrust mix

1. Combine chicken breasts, celery tops, onion, peppercorns, salt, chicken broth or bouillon cubes, and water in large frying pan; heat to boiling; cover
2. Simmer 30 minutes, or until chicken is tender. Remove from broth; cool until easy to handle. Strain broth into a 4-cup measure; add water, if needed, to make 1½ cups; then add cream.
•3. Pull skin from chicken and take meat from bones; cut meat into bite-size pieces. (There will be about 4 cups.) Spread chicken in an even layer in a shallow 8-cup baking dish; sprinkle pimiento over top.
4. Sauté celery and green pepper in butter or margarine 5 minutes in same large frying pan. Stir in flour, then broth mixture; cook, stirring constantly, until sauce thickens and boils 1 minute; remove from heat.
5. Stir in mushrooms and liquid and sherry; spoon over chicken mixture in baking dish. Keep hot in oven while making pastry.
6. Prepare piecrust mix, following label directions, or make your favorite single-crust recipe. Roll out to a rectangle or round 1 inch larger than baking dish; cut several slits in top to let steam escape. Place pastry over bubbling chicken mixture in dish; turn edge under, flush with rim.
7. Bake in hot oven (425°) 15 minutes or until bubbly and pastry is golden. Let stand 5 to 10 minutes before serving.

CHICKEN CASSEROLES

Casseroles are a boon to a homemaker because they are the best way to stretch smallish quantities of food to serve a family well. These baked dishes contain a medley of foods, usually meat with vegetables, noodles, or rice. Often a casserole is a whole meal in itself. It comes to the table in the dish in which it baked. Many casseroles have an additional virtue: you can do most of the preparation the day before, put the dish in the refrigerator, and then simply bake it before serving. For additional casserole recipes, see such special dishes as Chicken Risotto in the CHICKEN CONTINENTAL section, Arroz con Pollo Criollo and Mexicali Chicken in CHICKEN SOUTH-OF-THE-BORDER, Paella and Club Night Casserole in CHICKEN FOR A CROWD.

MOCK COQ AU VIN

Long slow cooking gives this aristocrat a mellow flavor. Its seasoning secrets: apple cider, mixed vegetable juices.

Bake at 350° for 2 hours and 15 minutes. Makes 4 servings.

1 stewing chicken (about 4 pounds), cut in serving-size pieces
¹/₃ cup flour
1¹/₂ teaspoons salt
3 tablespoons butter or margarine
¹/₂ cup diced cooked ham
12 small white onions, peeled
1 can (12 ounces) mixed vegetable juices (1¹/₂ cups)
1¹/₂ cups apple cider
1 can (3 or 4 ounces) mushroom caps
1 clove garlic, minced
6 peppercorns
6 whole cloves
1 bay leaf

1. Wash chicken pieces; pat dry. Shake with flour and salt in a paper bag to coat thoroughly.
2. Brown pieces, a few at a time, in butter or margarine in a large frying pan; place in a 12-cup baking dish; sprinkle with ham and top with onions.
3. Stir vegetable juices, cider, mushrooms and their liquid, and garlic into drippings in pan; heat to boiling, scraping brown bits from bottom of pan. Pour over chicken.
4. Tie seasonings in a tiny cheesecloth bag; add to casserole; cover.
5. Bake in moderate oven (350°) 2 hours and 15 minutes, or until chicken is very tender.
6. Uncover; remove spice bag and let chicken stand for 5 to 10 minutes, or until fat rises to top, then skim off. Garnish chicken with parsley, if you wish.

CHICKEN AND NOODLE CASSEROLE

Comforting, old family friend — always good and dependable.

Bake at 350° for 2 hours.

Makes 4 to 6 servings.

1 stewing chicken (4 to 5 pounds), cut into serving-size pieces
2 medium-size onions, chopped (1 cup)
1 tablespoon Worcestershire sauce
1 can condensed cream of mushroom soup
Hot noodles

1. Trim any excess fat from chicken pieces; remove skin from legs and breast.
2. Spread onion in bottom of a 12-cup baking dish; arrange chicken in 2 layers on top.
3. Stir Worcestershire sauce into soup in can; spoon over chicken; cover.
4. Bake in moderate oven (350°) 1 hour; uncover and stir to mix soup and chicken juices; cover again.
5. Bake 1 hour longer, or until chicken is very tender. Let casserole stand about 1 minute, or until fat rises to top; skim. Serve chicken with hot noodles, gravy.

CHICKEN MARENGO

This dish originated in the Italian town of Marengo; they say it was invented to serve to Napoleon.

Bake at 350° for 1½ hours.
Makes 8 servings.

6 slices bacon, cut in 1-inch pieces
2 broiler-fryers (about 2 pounds each), cut up
½ cup flour
2 teaspoons salt
¼ teaspoon pepper
2 medium-size onions, chopped (1 cup)
1 clove garlic, minced
1 can (3 or 4 ounces) whole mushrooms
2 cans (1 pound each) tomatoes
¼ cup chopped parsley
Few drops bottled red-pepper seasoning
1 cup Golden Croutons

1. Fry bacon until almost crisp in large frying pan. Lift out with slotted spoon; drain on paper towling and set aside for Step 6. Leave drippings in pan.
2. Wash and dry chicken pieces well. Snip off small rib bones with kitchen scissors, if you wish. Shake chicken in mixture of flour, salt, and pepper in paper bag to coat well. (Save any leftover flour mixture for Step 4.)
3. Brown chicken, a few pieces at a time, in bacon drippings; place in 12-cup shallow baking dish.
4. Sauté onion and garlic until soft in same frying pan; stir in saved flour mixture. Drain liquid from mushrooms. (Save mushrooms for Step 6.) Stir liquid, tomatoes, parsley, and red-pepper seasoning into frying pan; heat to boiling, stirring constantly.
5. Spoon over chicken in baking dish; cover. (Casserole can be put together up to this point, then chilled. Remove from refrigerator and let stand at room temperature 30 minutes before baking.)
6. Bake in moderate oven (350°) 1 hour and 20 minutes, or until chicken is tender. Uncover; sprinkle with saved bacon pieces and mushrooms. Bake 10 minutes longer, or until bacon is crisp.
7. Just before serving, sprinkle Golden Croutons over top; garnish with more chopped parsley, if you wish.
GOLDEN CROUTONS: Trim crusts from 2 slices of white bread; cut into 1½-inch cubes. Spread in single layer in shallow baking pan. Toast in moderate oven (350°) 10 minutes, or until golden. Makes 1 cup.

BRUNSWICK CHICKEN

This chicken dish includes corn, lima beans, a peppy tomato sauce.

Bake at 350° for 1½ hours.

Makes 8 servings.

2 broiler-fryers (about 2 pounds each), cut up
½ cup flour
1 envelope herb-salad-dressing mix
¼ cup shortening
1 large onion, chopped (1 cup)
1 tablespoon sugar
2 cans (about 1 pound each) tomatoes
1 package (10 ounces) frozen Fordhook lima beans, cooked and drained
1 package (10 ounces) frozen Fordhook lima beans, cooked and drained

1. Shake chicken in mixture of flour and salad-dressing mix in paper bag to coat well. Brown, a few pieces at a time, in shortening in large frying pan; arrange in a 12-cup baking dish.
2. Sauté onion in same frying pan; blend in any remaining seasoned flour, and sugar; stir in tomatoes. Heat to boiling, stirring constantly.
3. Spoon corn and lima beans around chicken in baking dish; pour tomato sauce over; cover with lid or foil; chill. Remove from refrigerator and let stand at room temperature 30 minutes before baking.
4. Bake in moderate oven (350°) 1½ hours, or until chicken is tender.

NEOPOLITAN CHICKEN

Families that love spaghetti will welcome this chicken-and-potatoes with spaghetti-sauce flavor.

Bake at 350° for 1½ hours.

Makes 6 servings.

2 broiler-fryers (about 2 pounds each), cut up
¼ cup flour
1 teaspoon salt
⅛ teaspoon pepper
2 tablespoons olive or salad oil
1 medium-size onion, chopped (½ cup)
1 clove garlic, minced
1 cup water
1 envelope spaghetti-sauce mix
3 medium-size tomatoes, chopped
¼ cup chopped parsley
6 medium-size potatoes, pared and cut in 1-inch cubes
1 large green pepper, seeded and cut into wide strips

1. Shake chicken with flour, salt, and pepper in paper bag to coat well. Brown, a few pieces at a time, in olive oil or salad oil in large frying pan; place in an 8-cup baking dish.
2. Sauté onion and garlic until softened in same frying pan; stir in water, then spaghetti-sauce mix; heat to boiling. Stir in tomatoes and parsley. Simmer, uncovered, 15 minutes.
3. Pour over chicken in baking dish; top with potato cubes and green pepper strips; cover.
4. Bake in moderate oven (350°) 1½ hours, or until chicken is tender.

SENEGALESE CHICKEN CASSEROLE

Mildly spiced with curry, chicken and noodles baked in a custard-type sauce.

Bake at 325° for 1 hour and 15 minutes. Makes 8 servings.

1 broiler-fryer (about 3 pounds)
1 small onion, sliced
Few celery tops
1¹/₂ teaspoons curry powder
2 teaspoons salt
¹/₈ teaspoon pepper
1¹/₂ cups water
Milk
1 package 8 ounces) fine noodles
1 package (10 ounces) frozen peas
1 can (5 ounces) toasted slivered almonds
4 eggs
1 cup cream for whipping

1. Combine chicken with onion, celery tops, curry powder, salt, pepper, and water in a large saucepan; cover. Simmer 45 minutes, or until tender.
2. Remove chicken from broth; cool until easy to handle. Strain broth into a 2-cup measure; skim any excess fat, then add milk, if needed, to make 2 cups; set aside for Step 5.
3. Pull skin from chicken and take meat from bones. Cut meat into bite-size pieces.
4. While fixing chicken, cook noodles and peas in separate saucepans, following label directions; drain. Combine with chicken and almonds in a buttered 10-cup baking dish.
5. Beat eggs slightly in a medium-size bowl; stir in the 2 cups chicken broth from Step 2 and cream. (This much can be done ahead.)
6. Pour custard mixture over chicken mixture, then stir lightly so liquid seeps to bottom. Bake in slow oven (325°) 1 hour and 15 minutes, or until custard sets. (Cover lightly with foil during last 15 minutes to keep top moist.) Garnish with diced red apple and coconut, if you wish.
MAKE-AHEAD NOTE: Cover chicken-noodle mixture in baking dish and custard mixture in bowl and chill. About 1¼ hours before serving combine both, following Step 6; place in a cold oven; set heat control at slow (325°). Bake 1 hour and 15 minutes.

CHICKEN AND ONIONS AU CASSEROLE

White meat and onions in a creamy sauce, with green peas mixed in like little gems.

Bake at 350° for 1½ hours.
Makes 8 servings.

1 package (8 ounces) medium noodles
1 package (9 ounces) frozen onions in
   cream sauce
2 cans condensed golden mushroom soup
1 package (10 ounces) frozen green peas
4 chicken breasts (about 12 ounces each)
Chopped pistachio nuts (optional)

1. Cook noodles, following label directions; drain. Combine with onions and 1 can of the mushroom soup in a greased shallow 12-cup baking dish; sprinkle with peas.
2. While noodles cook, pull skin from chicken breasts; cut each in half. Arrange in a single layer over peas; spread with remaining can of soup; cover.
3. Bake in moderate oven (350°) 1½ hours, or until chicken is tender and sauce is bubbly. Garnish with chopped pistachio nuts, if you wish.

DIXIE CHICKEN DINNER

A lively dish with layers of chicken, beans, olives, and tomatoes.

Bake at 350° for 1 hour.
Makes 8 servings.

2 broiler-fryers (about 2 pounds each)
³/₄ cup flour
2 teaspoons salt
1 teaspoon leaf basil, crumbled
4 tablespoons vegetable oil
2 cans (1 pound each) cooked dried lima
   beans
1 can (1 pound) cut green beans, drained
¹/₂ cup sliced stuffed green olives
¹/₂ cup sliced pitted ripe olives
4 medium-size firm ripe tomatoes, sliced
   ¹/₂ inch thick
1 clove garlic, minced
¹/₂ cup apple juice or water

green and ripe olives in a greased 12-cup shallow baking dish. Place tomato slices in a single layer over vegetables.
4. Pour all drippings from frying pan, then measure 4 tablespoonfuls and return to pan; stir in remaining ¼ cup flour and garlic; cook, stirring constantly, until bubbly.
5. Combine apple juice with saved bean liquid and additional water to make 2 cups; stir into flour mixture in frying pan. Continue cooking and stirring until sauce thickens and boils 1 minute; pour over vegetables in baking dish. Arrange browned chicken in a single layer on top, then press pieces down into vegetables slightly.
6. Bake in moderate oven (350°) 1 hour, or until chicken is tender and sauce bubbles up. Sprinkle with chopped parsley, if you wish.

1. Cut chicken into serving-size pieces. Shake pieces with a mixture of ½ cup flour, salt, and basil in a paper bag to coat evenly.
2. Brown slowly in vegetable oil in a large frying pan 10 minutes on each side; remove and set aside.
3. While chicken browns, drain liquid from lima beans into a 2-cup measure; combine limas with green beans, and

CHICKEN SALADS

Salads are those hit-the-spot dishes for times when your appetite is jaded. One way salads invite and arouse the senses is by *looking* so pretty. On a hot summer day, on a tired evening, at any time when a light meal is in order, chicken salad can be the perfect answer. Besides the dozen salads here, don't miss the special Molded Chicken Indienne in COMPANY'S COMING, Chinese Chicken Salad in ORIENTAL CHICKEN, and Chicken and Fruit Harmony in CHICKEN FOR A CROWD, plus the salads in LEFTOVER CHICKEN.

CHICKEN-CORN SALAD

Filling fare with all white meat chicken, hard-cooked eggs, corn nuggets, and tender macaroni.

Makes 6 servings.

2 chicken breasts (about 12 ounces each)
2 cups water
1 slice onion
Few celery tops
1¹/₄ teaspoons salt
3 tablespoons cider vinegar
2 teaspoons sugar
¹/₄ teaspoon pepper
¹/₂ cup vegetable oil
1 package (8 ounces) small macaroni shells
1 can (12 or 16 ounces) whole-kernel corn, well drained
1 cup thinly sliced celery
1 large head Boston lettuce
3 hard-cooked eggs, shelled and coarsely chopped
¹/₄ cup mayonnaise or salad dressing
3 tablespoons chopped parsley

1. Combine chicken breasts with water, onion, celery tops, and ¼ teaspoon of the salt in a medium-size saucepan; cover. Simmer 30 minutes, or until chicken is tender. Remove from broth and cool until easy to handle. (Save broth to add to soup for another day.)
2. Pull skin from chicken and take meat from bones; cut meat into bite-size pieces.
3. Combine vinegar, sugar, remaining 1 teaspoon salt, pepper, and vegetable oil in a jar with a tight fitting lid; shake well to mix. Drizzle 1 tablespoon over chicken; chill.
4. Cook macaroni in boiling salted water, following label directions; drain well. Combine with corn, celery, and 1 tablespoon of the dressing in a large bowl; toss to mix well; chill. (Set remaining dressing aside for Step 7.)
5. When ready to serve, line 6 soup plates or shallow salad bowls with lettuce; shred remaining lettuce into pieces in centers. Spoon macaroni mixture on top.
6. Add chopped eggs to chicken mixture; toss lightly to mix; spoon over macaroni.
7. Beat remaining dressing into mayonnaise or salad dressing and parsley in a small bowl; pass separately.

Quick and Easy

BARBECUED CHICKEN SUPPER SALAD

You can use ready-cooked meat and salad from your supermarket for this hearty hot-weather meal.

Makes 4 servings.

2 containers (1 pound each) prepared macaroni salad
1 package (4 ounces) shredded Cheddar cheese
1 can (8 ounces) lima beans, drained
1/2 cup chopped celery
1/2 teaspoon fines herbes
1 small head chicory, washed, drained
2 medium-size tomatoes, cut in wedges
2 ready-to-eat barbecued chickens, weighing about 2 pounds each
Sweet mixed pickles
Stuffed green olives

1. Combine macaroni salad, cheese, lima beans, celery, and herbes in a large bowl; toss lightly to mix well. Chill about an hour to season.
2. Just before serving, line a large platter with chicory leaves; break remaining into bite-size pieces in center; spoon macaroni salad on top. Tuck tomato wedges around salad.
3. Cut chickens in half with kitchen scissors; place, skin side up, around edge of platter.
4. Thread pickles and olives, alternately, onto wooden picks; stick, kebab style, into macaroni salad. Serve with rye bread-and-butter sandwiches, if you wish.

CHICKEN VERONIQUE

Fresh green grapes and apricots, plus a tangy cucumber dressing, add style to a salad favorite.

Makes 6 servings.

4 chicken breasts (about 12 ounces each)
Few celery tops
2 teaspoons salt
6 peppercorns
1 bay leaf
1 envelope instant chicken broth
  OR 1 chicken bouillon cube
1 cup water
1 cup chopped celery
1 cup seedless green grapes, halved
2 cups Cucumber Dressing
Bibb lettuce
6 apricots, washed, halved, and pitted

1. Combine chicken breasts, celery tops, salt, peppercorns, bay leaf, instant chicken broth or bouillon cube, and water in a large frying pan; heat to boiling; cover. Simmer 30 minutes, until meat is tender.
2. Cool in broth until easy to handle, then remove and pull off skin; take meat from bones; cube. Place in a large bowl. (Strain broth and chill for making soup another day.)
3. Add celery and grapes to chicken; drizzle with about half of the Cucumber Dressing; toss lightly to mix. Chill at least an hour to season.
4. When ready to serve, line a large bowl with lettuce; pile chicken mixture in center; frame with apricot halves. Serve with remaining dressing.

CUCUMBER DRESSING: Combine 6 tablespoons mayonnaise or salad dressing, 1½ teaspoons salt, 1 teaspoon chopped fresh dill, ¼ teaspoon pepper, 6 tablespoons lemon juice, and 1 cup buttermilk in a small bowl; beat until well-blended. Stir in 1 small cucumber, pared, diced, and drained well. Chill at least an hour to season. Makes about 2 cups.

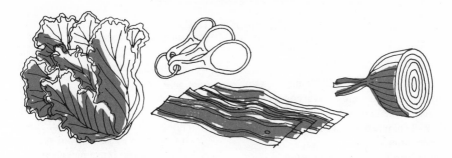

CURRIED CHICKEN SALAD PUFFS

A ladies' luncheon delight: Golden popovers halved and filled with faintly curried chicken salad.

Makes about 6 cups.

4 chicken breasts (about 12 ounces each)
1 small onion, sliced
Handful of celery tops
3 teaspoons salt
6 peppercorns
1¹/₂ cups water
2 cups chopped celery
1¹/₄ cups mayonnaise or salad dressing
1 teaspoon curry powder
1 teaspoon sugar
2 teaspoons grated onion
2 teaspoons lemon juice
6 popovers
6 slices bacon
6 leaves Boston lettuce

1. Simmer chicken breasts, covered, with sliced onion, celery tops, 2 teaspoons of the salt, peppercorns, and water in a kettle 30 minutes, or until chicken is tender. (Remaining salt is for salad in Step 4.)
2. Remove chicken from broth; cool until easy to handle. (Chill broth to use for soup another day.) Pull skin from chicken and take meat from bones; dice meat; chill.
3. When ready to finish salad, combine chicken and celery in a large bowl.
4. Blend mayonnaise or salad dressing, curry powder, sugar, remaining 1 teaspoon salt, grated onion, and lemon juice in a small bowl; spoon over chicken; toss to mix well. Chill.
5. Sauté bacon until almost crisp in a large frying pan; roll each slice around the tines of a fork to make a curl; drain on paper toweling.
6. Cut popovers in half lengthwise; line half of each with lettuce, then fill with chicken salad, dividing evenly. Garnish with bacon curls and serve with remaining popover halves.

POPOVERS

Bake at 400° for 50 minutes.
Makes 6 popovers.

3 eggs
1 cup milk
1 cup sifted regular flour
¹/₂ teaspoon salt

1. Beat eggs just until foamy in a medium-size bowl; add milk, flour, and salt all at once; beat briskly ½ minute. Scrape down side of bowl; beat 1½ minutes longer. (Batter will be thin and smooth.)
2. Pour into 6 well-greased 6-ounce custard cups, filling each ⅔ full. Set cups, not touching, in a shallow pan.
3. Bake in hot oven (400°) 50 minutes, or until puffed and golden brown; remove from cups. Poke a small hole in side of each to let steam escape; place on wire rack to cool.

WINTER CHICKEN SALAD

White meat, carrots, and celery team up in a warm salad for cold weather.

Makes 6 servings.

3 chicken breasts (about 12 ounces each)
1 pound carrots, pared and sliced thin
2 cups sliced celery
1 small onion, chopped (1/4 cup)
1/4 cup water
1 envelope instant chicken broth
  OR 1 chicken bouillon cube
2 teaspoons salt
1/2 cup mayonnaise or salad dressing
Potato chips

1. Pull skin from chicken breasts, then cut meat from bones; dice meat.
2. Combine with carrots, celery, onion, water, chicken broth or bouillon cube, and salt in a large frying pan; heat to boiling; cover.
3. Simmer 30 minutes, or until chicken is tender. Drain off any broth and save to add to soup or stew. Fold mayonnaise or salad dressing into chicken mixture.
4. Spoon onto a large serving platter; frame with potato chips and garnish with parsley, if you wish.

CHICKEN MOUSSE

Make this lovely mold at leisure in the evening to serve triumphantly to guests the next day.

Makes 6 servings.

2 chicken breasts (about 12 ounces each)
1 small onion, sliced
Handful of celery tops
1 teaspoon salt
3 peppercorns
2 packages (3 ounces each) mixed
  vegetable flavor gelatin
1 cup hot water
2 tablespoons lemon juice
4 radishes
1 can condensed cream of chicken soup
1/2 cup mayonnaise or salad dressing
1 cup diced celery
1/4 cup chopped toasted slivered almonds
  (from a 5-ounce can)
1 tablespoon cut chives

1. Simmer chicken breasts, covered, with onion, celery tops, salt, peppercorns, and 1 cup water in a medium-size saucepan 30 minutes, or until chicken is tender. Remove from broth and cool until easy to handle. Strain broth into a 2-cup measure; add water, if needed, to make 1 cup; set aside until needed for Step 6.

2. Pull skin from chicken and take meat from bones; dice meat and set aside.
3. Dissolve both packages of gelatin in hot water in a large bowl; stir in lemon juice. Measure 1/4 cup into a 6-cup mold; stir in 1/2 cup cold water.
4. Place mold in a pan of ice and water to speed setting; chill until as thick as unbeaten egg white. Keep bowl of remaining gelatin mixture at room temperature for Step 6.
5. While layer chills, trim radishes, leaving about an inch of green leafy tops on each; cut radishes into roses. Arrange in thickened gelatin in mold; continue chilling until sticky-firm.
6. Beat soup, the 1 cup chicken broth, and mayonnaise or salad dressing into remaining gelatin mixture in bowl; chill until as thick as unbeaten egg white.
7. Fold in diced chicken, celery, almonds, and chives; carefully spoon over sticky-firm radish layer. Remove from ice and water; chill in refrigerator several hours, or until firm. (Overnight is best.)
8. When ready to serve, unmold onto a large serving plate. Frame with more radish roses and sprigs of endive or chicory, if you wish.

CURRIED CHICKEN CORONET

A partylike rich chicken-salad mousse delicately spiced with curry.

Makes 8 servings.

2 **whole chicken breasts (about 2 pounds)**
2 **cups water**
1 **medium-size onion, sliced**
Handful of celery tops
1½ **teaspoons salt**
3 **peppercorns**
1 **envelope unflavored gelatin**
2 **eggs, separated**
½ **cup chopped toasted almonds**
1 **teaspoon curry powder**
¼ **teaspoon pepper**
1 **cup mayonnaise**
1 **cup cream for whipping**
1 **can (about 13 ounces) frozen pineapple**
   chunks, thawed and drained
½ **cup flaked coconut**

1. Combine chicken breasts, water, onion, celery tops, 1 teaspoon salt, and peppercorns in large saucepan; simmer, covered, 45 minutes, or until chicken is tender. Let stand until cool enough to handle, then skin chicken and take meat from bones. Dice chicken fine (you should have about 2 cups diced chicken).

2. Strain stock into a bowl; measure out 1 cupful; pour into a medium-size saucepan and cool. (Save any remaining stock for soup for another day.)

3. Soften gelatin in cooled stock in saucepan; heat, stirring constantly, just until dissolved.

4. Beat egg yolks slightly in small bowl; slowly stir in dissolved gelatin. Return mixture to saucepan and cook, stirring constantly, 1 minute, or until slightly thickened; remove from heat.

5. Stir in diced chicken, almonds, curry powder, ½ teaspoon salt, and pepper, blending well. Chill 30 minutes, or until mixture is syrupy-thick; blend in mayonnaise.

6. Beat egg whites until stiff in large bowl; fold in chicken mixture until no streaks of white remain.

7. Beat cream until stiff in medium-size bowl; fold into chicken mixture.

8. Pour into a 6-cup ring mold; chill several hours, or until firm.

9. Unmold onto serving plate; fit a shallow bowl into center of mold; fill with pineapple chunks; sprinkle with coconut.

AVOCADO CHICKEN SALAD

Chilled, seasoned chicken and delicate avocado: a combination everybody loves.

Makes 6 servings.

1 **stewing chicken (about 4 pounds), cooked**
4 **tablespoons salad oil**
2 **tablespoons fresh lime juice**
¼ **teaspoon ground ginger**
1 **large head of iceberg lettuce, washed and**
   dried
1 **cup sliced celery**
1 **large ripe avocado**

1. Cool chicken until easy to handle; remove skin and white and dark meat from frame in chunks as big as possible, then slice into thin bite-size pieces. (You should have about 4 cups.) Place in medium-size bowl. Save broth for making soup another day.

2. Combine salad oil, lime juice, and ginger in a cup; sprinkle over chicken; toss to coat well; cover; chill.

3. At serving time, place a large lettuce leaf on each plate; shred remaining lettuce; toss with celery, and divide evenly onto lettuce leaves. Top with mounds of marinated chicken.

4. Peel avocado, remove seed, and cut into thin lengthwise slices; arrange 3 on top of each mound of chicken to garnish.

CHICKEN SALAD SOUFFLES

Delicately seasoned and rich little main-dish salads are good summer or winter.
Makes 6 servings.

1 stewing chicken (5 pounds), cut up
6 cups water
1 small onion, sliced
Few celery tops
3 teaspoons salt
6 peppercorns
2 envelopes unflavored gelatin
1/2 cup apple juice
1 cup mayonnaise or salad dressing
1/2 cup thinly sliced celery
1/4 cup toasted slivered almonds, chopped
1/4 cup chopped stuffed green olives
Boston lettuce

1. Combine chicken, water, onion, celery tops, salt, and peppercorns in a kettle; cover. Simmer 2 hours, or until chicken is very tender; remove from broth. Strain broth into a 4-cup measure.
2. Soften gelatin in apple juice in a medium-size saucepan; stir in 3 cups of the broth. (Chill any remaining broth to add to soup for another meal.)
3. Heat gelatin mixture slowly, stirring constantly, until gelatin dissolves. Cool.
4. Pull skin from chicken and take meat from bones; dice fine. (There should be about 4 cups.)
5. Blend mayonnaise or salad dressing into gelatin mixture in saucepan; pour into 2 ice-cube trays or a pan, 8x8x2. Freeze 20 minutes, or just until firm about 1 inch in from edges.
6. Spoon into a chilled large bowl; beat until fluffy thick. Fold in diced chicken, celery, almonds, and olives. Spoon into 6 individual molds. (Or use a large 6-cup mold.) Chill several hours or until firm.
7. When ready to serve, unmold onto lettuce-lined plates. Garnish with stuffed green olive slices, honeydew melon balls and crescents, and sprigs of watercress.

JELLIED CHICKEN LOAF

A perfect make-ahead to perk up wilted appetites on a warm day.
Makes 6 to 8 servings.

1 stewing chicken (5 to 6 pounds), not cut up
1 medium-size onion, sliced
2 teaspoons salt
1 teaspoon peppercorns
Handful of celery tops
2 1/2 cups water
1 envelope unflavored gelatin
2 hard-cooked eggs, shelled and sliced
Parsley
1 tablespoon prepared mustard
1/2 cup sour cream

1. Simmer chicken with onion, salt, peppercorns, celery tops, and water in a large kettle, covered, 2 hours or until tender. Let stand in broth until cool.
2. Strain broth into a 4-cup measure; skim off any fat that rises to top, then add enough water to make 3 cups; cool.
3. Pull all chicken from frame; trim off any fat and skin; chop meat finely. (You should have about 4 cups.) Spoon into a 6-cup loaf pan.
4. Soften gelatin in 1 cup of the cooled broth in a small saucepan; heat, stirring constantly, just until dissolved. Stir back into remaining broth; pour over chicken in loaf pan, pressing chicken down with a fork until completely covered (mixture should just fill pan).
5. Chill 5 to 6 hours or overnight, or until the loaf is firm enough to slice.
6. Unmold onto serving plate; garnish with sliced hard-cooked eggs and parsley. Slice and serve with prepared mustard blended into the sour cream.

PATIO CHICKEN BOWL

4 cups cubed cooked chicken (can be from a 5-pound stewing chicken)
1 cup sliced celery
¹/₃ cup mayonnaise or salad dressing
2 tablespoons lemon juice
2 teaspoons grated onion
1 teaspoon salt
1 head romaine
1 cup cantaloupe balls
¹/₂ pound seedless grapes (1 cup)
¹/₄ cup toasted slivered almonds

It would be hard to come up with a prettier or more appetizing summer meal. Sunny cantaloupe balls and green grapes ring salad-seasoned chicken with almonds. Makes 6 servings.

1. Combine chicken, celery, mayonnaise or salad dressing, lemon juice, onion, and salt in a medium-size bowl; toss to mix. Cover; chill at least an hour to season.
2. When ready to serve, break romaine into bite-size pieces; place in bottom of large bowl. Spoon chicken salad over; pile cantaloupe balls in center, ring edge with grapes, sprinkle almonds between.

PARISIAN CHICKEN BOWL

*Halved chicken breasts are glazed, French style, and served cold with seasoned vegetables for this fancy bowl.
Makes 6 servings.*

3 whole chicken breasts (12 ounces each)
1 small onion, sliced
1 teaspoon salt
¹/₈ teaspoon pepper
1 bay leaf
2 cups water
1 envelope unflavored gelatin
¹/₂ cup mayonnaise or salad dressing
6 pitted ripe olives
1 package (10 ounces) frozen Fordhook lima beans
¹/₂ cup bottled Italian salad dressing
4 cups broken mixed salad greens
3 medium-size tomatoes, peeled and sliced
3 hard-cooked eggs, shelled and quartered

1. Combine chicken breasts with onion, salt, pepper, bay leaf, and water in a large saucepan; cover. Simmer 30 minutes, or just until tender.
2. Remove from broth, cool until easy to handle, then pull off skin. Remove meat from each half of breast in one piece; place in one layer in a shallow dish. Chill.
3. Strain broth into a 2-cup measure; chill just until fat rises to top, then skim.
4. Soften gelatin in 1 cup of the broth in

a small saucepan. (Save any remaining to add to soup.) Heat gelatin mixture, stirring constantly, just until gelatin dissolves; pour into a small bowl. Blend in mayonnaise or salad dressing; chill, stirring several times, 20 minutes, or until as thick as unbeaten egg white.
5. Spoon part over chilled chicken breasts to make a thick layer, then repeat with remaining until chicken is evenly glazed. Cut each olive into 6 slivers, arrange, petal fashion, on top of each glazed chicken breast; chill until gelatin is firm.
6. Cook lima beans, following label directions; drain. Toss with ¼ cup of the Italian dressing in a small bowl; cover. (This much can be done early in the day, or even a day ahead.)
7. When ready to serve, place salad greens in a large shallow bowl; drizzle remaining ¼ cup Italian dressing over; toss lightly to mix. Top with tomato slices; mound lima beans in center, then arrange chicken breasts, spoke fashion, around beans; place quartered eggs around edge of bowl. Garnish with a cherry-tomato flower, if you wish. To make, cut a cherry tomato into eights from tip almost to stem end; separate "petals" slightly; stuff with a ripe olive and top with a sprig of parsley.

PICNIC CHICK

Plan a picnic and instantly someone will say, "Let's have fried chicken!" Here are four recipes for luscious chicken that's especially suitable to take along to eat outdoors with the fingers. (Best way to pack chicken, by the way, is in a large shallow pan or box lined with paper toweling and covered tightly.) For variety's sake, here also are two recipes for picnicky chicken sandwiches; others can be found in the section on SANDWICHES.

CHICKEN DOUBLE-DECKERS

Fat sandwiches of Italian bread, filled with avocado spread and fruited meat salad.

Makes 16 sandwiches.

1 broiler-fryer (about 2¹/₂ pounds)
1 cup water
1¹/₂ teaspoons salt
Few celery tops
1 can (about 9 ounces) pineapple tidbits
¹/₂ cup halved green grapes
1 cup mayonnaise or salad dressing
1 medium-size firm ripe avocado
6 slices crisp bacon, crumbled
2 loaves Italian bread

1. Combine chicken with water, 1 teaspoon salt, and celery tops in a large saucepan; heat to boiling; cover. Simmer 1 hour, or until tender.
2. Remove from broth and cool until easy to handle; strain broth and chill for soup or gravy. Pull skin from chicken and take meat from bones; dice. (There should be about 2 cups.) Place in a medium-size bowl.
3. Drain syrup from pineapple into a cup. Add pineapple and grapes to chicken. Blend 2 tablespoons of the syrup with ¹/₂ cup mayonnaise or salad dressing and remaining ¹/₂ teaspoon salt in a small bowl; fold into chicken mixture. Chill.
4. Halve avocado; pit and peel. Mash in a small bowl; stir in crumbled bacon, ¹/₄ cup of the remaining mayonnaise or salad dressing, and red pepper seasoning. (Fix avocado mixture no longer than an hour ahead so that it keeps its bright color.)
5. Cut each loaf of bread lengthwise into 3 even slices; spread with remaining ¹/₄ cup mayonnaise or salad dressing.
6. Spread avocado mixture on bottom slices and chicken salad on middle slices; stack loaves back in shape; cover with top slices. Cut loaf crosswise into 8 thick double-decker sandwiches.

CHICKEN JUMBOS

White meat and pineapple in a creamy dressing on raisin bread make delicious stay-moist picnic sandwiches.

Makes 4 sandwiches.

1 can (about 1 pound, 5 ounces)
   pineapple spears
16 thin slices cooked chicken breast
8 slices unfrosted cinnamon-raisin
   bread, buttered
1/4 cup mayonnaise or salad dressing
2 tablespoons chopped pecans

1. Drain syrup from pineapple into a cup; set aside for Step 3.
2. Arrange chicken slices and pineapple spears, overlapping, on each of 4 slices of bread.
3. Blend mayonnaise or salad dressing, 1 tablespoon of the pineapple syrup, and pecans in a cup; spoon a generous tea-spoonful over filling for each sandwich. Cover with remaining slices of bread. (Chill remaining pineapple syrup to add to a breakfast beverage.)
4. Place each sandwich in a plastic bag, or wrap in foil or transparent wrap.

FOURTH OF JULY CHICKEN

The kind of fried chicken everybody loves, unadorned and crisp for finger eating.

Makes 8 servings.

2 broiler-fryers (2½ to 3 pounds), cut up
   in serving-size pieces
1 cup flour
2½ teaspoons salt
½ teaspoon onion salt
1 cup shortening
1 cup water

1. Dip each piece of chicken in flour mixed with salt and onion salt.
2. Brown, a few pieces at a time, in hot shortening in a large, heavy skillet.
3. Pile all chicken pieces in the skillet, lower heat, and cook, covered, 35 to 40 minutes, turning frequently.
4. Add water and cover pan again. Cook another 15 minutes, or until liquid has been absorbed.
5. Drain chicken pieces on paper toweling and cool until ready for the picnic hamper.

ROSEMARY CHICKEN

Serve this flavory chicken on the patio for a summer supper.
Bake at 400° for 1 hour.
Makes 4 servings.
2 broiler-fryers (2 pounds each), cut up
1 large onion, cut into thick slices
2/3 cup catsup
1/3 cup vinegar
4 tablespoons (½ stick) butter or
   margarine
1 clove garlic, minced
1 teaspoon rosemary, crushed
1 teaspoon salt
1/4 teaspoon dry mustard

1. Place chicken, skin side down, in a single layer in a buttered shallow baking pan; top with onion slices.
2. Mix remaining ingredients in a small saucepan; heat to boiling; pour over chicken.
3. Bake in hot oven (400°) 30 minutes. Turn chicken, skin side up; baste with sauce in pan. Continue baking, basting once or twice, 30 minutes longer, or until tender and richly glazed.

SIMPLE SIMON

Chicken baked in a cheese-cracker coating — delicious hot or cold.

Bake at 375° for 1 hour.

Makes 6 servings.

1 package (about 6 ounces) cheese
    crackers, crushed fine
2 teaspoons seasoned salt
1/2 cup salad oil
2 broiler-fryers (about 3 pounds each),
    cut in serving-size pieces

1. Place cracker crumbs in a pie plate; stir in seasoned salt. Pour salad oil into a second pie plate.
2. Dip chicken pieces into salad oil, then into crushed crumbs to coat well. Place in a single layer in an ungreased large shallow pan.
3. Bake in moderate oven (375°) 1 hour, or until tender and golden-brown. Serve warm or cold.

DUNKING CHICKEN

Fine finger food — crackly crisp outside, juicy inside — for picnic or patio meals.

Makes 6 servings.

2 broiler-fryers (about 2 pounds each),
    cut up
1 cup flour
2 teaspoons salt
1/2 teaspoon pepper
Bacon drippings
Orange Curry Dunk
Zippy Tomato Dunk

1. Wash and dry chicken pieces well. Shake in mixture of flour, salt, and pepper in paper bag to coat well.
2. Heat bacon drippings in large frying pan or electric skillet. It'll take about 1 cup, for fat should be about ½ inch deep. (If you like, use part shortening.)
3. Place chicken in a single layer in hot fat; cover lightly. Cook over *low heat* 20 minutes, or until golden; turn; cover again and cook 20 minutes to brown other side. (If using an electric skillet, follow manufacturer's directions.) Remove browned chicken and set aside while cooking any remaining pieces, adding more drippings, if needed, to keep fat ½ inch deep.
4. Drain fat from frying pan, leaving just enough to keep chicken from sticking; return all chicken to pan. Cover;

cook, turning once or twice, over very low heat 30 minutes longer, or until tender.
5. Serve hot or cold, with dunking sauces.

ORANGE CURRY DUNK
Makes 2 cups.

1 cup orange marmalade
1/3 cup vinegar
1/4 cup granulated sugar
2 tablespoons brown sugar
1 tablespoon curry powder
1 tablespoon Worcestershire sauce
1 teaspoon salt
1/2 teaspoon ground ginger

Combine all ingredients in small saucepan; heat to boiling, then simmer, stirring constantly, until marmalade is melted and sauce is blended. Serve warm or cold.

ZIPPY TOMATO DUNK
Makes 1½ cups.

1 can (8 ounces) tomato sauce
1/2 cup finely chopped green pepper
1/2 cup finely chopped celery
2 tablespoons vinegar
2 tablespoons light molasses
1 tablespoon Worcestershire sauce
1/4 teaspoon bottled red-pepper seasoning

Combine all ingredients in small saucepan; heat to boiling, then simmer, stirring constantly, 5 minutes, or until vegetables are softened and sauce is blended.

Rosemary Chicken

Chicken Perfection

"COMPANY'S COMING" CHICKEN

The most convincing way to make guests feel honored is to serve them something special, something delicious that says, "You are not only Welcome, but Important." A company dinner is also the time to show off your virtuosity as a cook and enhance your reputation as a skillful hostess. The creative chicken dishes here will carry your message. If you're looking for something especially exotic, turn also to CONTINENTAL CHICKEN or one of the other foreign-dish sections. And if you are expecting to serve more than eight, try a recipe from CHICKEN FOR A CROWD.

APPLE CIDER CHICKEN

This chicken-in-sauce makes a fine company dinner served over hot buttered noodles.

Makes 4 servings.

1 broiler-fryer (about 3 pounds), cut in
   serving-size pieces
6 tablespoons flour
¹/₄ cup salad oil
1 small onion, sliced and separated
   into rings
¹/₂ clove garlic, minced
1 envelope instant chicken broth
¹/₂ teaspoon salt
¹/₈ teaspoon pepper
¹/₂ cup apple cider
¹/₂ cup water
2 tablespoons catsup
1 teaspoon grated lemon rind

1. Wash chicken pieces; pat dry. Shake, a few at a time, in 4 tablespoons of the flour in a paper bag to coat well. (Save remaining flour for sauce in Step 3).
2. Brown chicken slowly in salad oil in a large frying pan; remove from pan and set aside for Step 4.
3. Stir onion and garlic into drippings in pan; sauté just until soft. Blend in saved 2 tablespoons flour, chicken broth, salt, and pepper; cook, stirring all the time, just until mixture bubbles. Stir in cider, water, catsup, and lemon rind; continue cooking and stirring until sauce thickens and boils 1 minute.
4. Return chicken to pan; cover. Simmer 45 minutes or until tender.

CHICKEN IMPERIAL

A bit of a production to make, but a splendid dish to serve. And if guests are late, this dinner will wait.

Bake at 350° for 1 hour and 15 minutes. Makes 8 servings.

- **2 cups soft bread crumbs (4 slices)**
- **³/₄ cup finely diced cooked ham**
- **¹/₂ cup chopped parsley**
- **8 tablespoons (1 stick) hard butter or margarine, sliced thin**
- **4 chicken breasts (about 12 ounces each)**
- **4 chicken drumsticks with thighs**
- **1 cup milk**
- **1 cup fine dry bread crumbs**
- **1 can or 1 envelope (2 to a package) cream of mushroom soup mix**
- **2 cups cold water**
- **¹/₄ cup chili sauce**

1. Mix soft bread crumbs, ham, and parsley in a large bowl; cut in butter or margarine quickly with a pastry blender; chill while fixing chicken so butter doesn't melt.
2. Pull skin from chicken pieces; halve breasts, then cut out rib bones with scissors. Separate thighs and drumsticks at joints with a sharp knife. To make pockets for stuffing, pull each breast piece open on its thick side, and cut an opening along bone in each leg and thigh.
3. Stuff about ¼ cup chilled stuffing into each half breast and 2 tablespoonfuls into each leg and thigh.
4. Place ½ cup of the milk in a pie plate and dry bread crumbs on a sheet of waxed paper. (Set remaining ½ cup milk aside for making sauce.) Roll stuffed chicken pieces in milk, then in bread crumbs to coat; chill while making sauce.
5. Combine mushroom soup mix and water in a small saucepan; cook, following label directions. Stir in remaining ½ cup milk and chili sauce; pour 1 cup into shallow 12-cup baking dish.
6. Place chicken pieces, standing on edge if needed to fit, in sauce in dish; drizzle remaining sauce between pieces.
7. Bake in moderate oven (350°) 1 hour and 15 minutes, or until tender and richly golden. Garnish with parsley, if you wish.

HOSTESS NOTE: If dinner is delayed, simply lower oven heat to very slow (250°) and fit a sheet of foil, tent fashion, over casserole. It will hold about an hour.

PIMIENTO CHICKEN

Quick and Easy

Tangy but not fiery, little canned peppers add zip and color to a chicken dish. Makes 4 servings.

- **4 tablespoons butter or margarine**
- **1 broiler-fryer (about 2¹/₂ pounds), cut up**
- **1 teaspoon salt**
- **¹/₂ teaspoon paprika**
- **¹/₄ pound mushrooms, sliced**
- **2 tablespoons flour**
- **1 small onion, chopped (¹/₄ cup)**
- **2 cups condensed chicken broth**
- **¹/₂ cup light cream**
- **1 jar (4 ounces) pimientos, chopped**
- **1 tablespoon parsley, chopped**

1. Heat butter or margarine in a heavy skillet. Add chicken, sprinkle with salt and paprika, and brown on both sides.
2. Lower heat, add mushrooms, and sauté 5 minutes.
3. Stir in the flour, onion, and broth. Simmer, covered, 30 minutes.
4. Stir in the cream, pimientos, and parsley, and simmer 5 minutes more. Serve over hot noodles.

CHICKEN IN ORANGE SAUCE

This luscious concoction can be made the day before, with last-minute touches added just before guests arrive.

Makes 4 servings.

1 broiler-fryer (about 3 pounds), cut in serving-size pieces
1/2 cup (1 stick) butter or margarine
1/4 cup flour
2 tablespoons brown sugar
1 teaspoon salt
1/2 teaspoon ground ginger
1/8 teaspoon pepper
1 1/2 cups orange juice
1/2 cup water
2 oranges, pared and sectioned

1. Wash chicken pieces; pat dry. Brown slowly in butter or margarine in large frying pan; remove from pan and set aside for Step 3.
2. Blend flour, brown sugar, salt, ginger, and pepper into drippings in pan; cook, stirring all the time, just until mixture bubbles. Stir in orange juice and water slowly; continue cooking and stirring un-til sauce thickens and boils 1 minute; remove from heat.
3. Return chicken to pan; cool. Cover and chill (this much can be done the day before).
4. About 45 minutes before serving time, reheat chicken and sauce just to boiling, then simmer, covered, 30 minutes. Lay orange sections around chicken; continue cooking 15 minutes longer, or until chicken is tender. Serve with fluffy hot rice seasoned with chopped parsley, if you wish.

CRISP CORNISH HENS

Midget chickens in coats of seasoned crumbs bake themselves to a golden turn.

Bake at 350° for 1 1/4 hours.
Makes 6 servings.

6 frozen Rock Cornish hens (about 1 pound each), thawed
Salt
1/2 cup buttermilk
2 packages seasoned coating mix for chicken
1 package (1 pound) spinach noodles
1/2 teaspoon onion salt
2 tablespoons butter or margarine

1. Remove giblets from Cornish hens and chill or freeze to simmer for gravy another day. Rinse hens inside and out; pat dry. Sprinkle cavities lightly with salt.
2. Brush hens, one at a time, with buttermilk, then shake in coating mix. Place, breast side up and not touching, in a jelly-roll pan.
3. Bake in moderate oven (350°) for 1 1/4 hours, or until tender and golden.
4. While hens bake, cook noodles in a kettle, following label directions; drain; return to kettle. Add onion salt and butter or margarine; toss lightly to mix.
5. Spoon noodles onto a large deep serving platter; arrange Cornish hens on top. Garnish with sprigs of watercress.

ELEGANT CHICKEN WITH CASHEWS

Here's a rich dish for special guests, a favorite of young hostesses. Keep the rest of the meal simple. Makes 4 servings.

¹/₂ cup fresh mushrooms, sliced
1 large (or 1¹/₂ medium) green pepper, coarsely chopped
8 tablespoons (1 stick) butter
2 cups diced cooked chicken OR 2 cans (5 ounces each) boned chicken, diced
1 can (3 or 4 ounces) sliced pimientos, drained
¹/₂ cup plus 2 tablespoons dry sherry
2 cups light cream
2 egg yolks
¹/₂ teaspoon nutmeg
Salt and white pepper to taste
1 cup salted cashews, split and toasted

1. Sauté mushrooms and peppers in butter for 5 to 10 minutes or until tender.
2. Add chicken, pimientos, ¹/₂ cup sherry, and simmer, covered, until sherry is completely absorbed — 8 to 10 minutes. Lower heat and stir in cream; let cook for 5 minutes.
3. Stir in egg yolks to thicken sauce. Season with nutmeg, salt, and white pepper.
4. Turn into serving dish and sprinkle with 2 tablespoons sherry and the cashews. Serve at once.

CHICKEN PERFECTION

Chicken baked with this spicy sweet-sour glaze can best be described as gorgeous. Bake at 400° about 1 hour.

Makes 8 servings.

Curry Glaze
2 broiler-fryers (about 3 pounds each), quartered
6 tablespoons flour
1¹/₂ teaspoons salt
1 teaspoon ground ginger
6 tablespoons (³/₄ stick) butter or margarine
Buttered hot rice

1. Make Curry Glaze.
2. Cut away backbones and any small rib bones from chickens. (Kitchen scissors do a fast neat job.) Pull off skin, if desired. Shake chicken pieces in mixture of flour, salt, and ginger in paper bag to coat well.
3. Melt butter or margarine in large shallow baking or roasting pan. Roll chicken in melted butter to coat well, then arrange, skin side up, in single layer in pan.
4. Bake, uncovered, in hot oven (400°) 20 minutes, or until beginning to turn golden. Spoon about half of Curry Glaze on top of chicken to make a thick coating; bake 20 minutes. Spoon on remaining glaze; bake 20 minutes longer, or until chicken is tender and richly browned.
5. Arrange chicken around a mound of buttered hot rice on serving platter. Garnish with lemon cups filled with your own or store-bought pepper relish, if you wish.

CURRY GLAZE
Makes about 2 cups.

1 medium-size onion, chopped (¹/₂ cup)
6 slices bacon, finely diced
2 tablespoons flour
1 tablespoon curry powder
1 tablespoon sugar
1 can condensed beef broth
2 tablespoons flaked coconut
2 tablespoons applesauce
2 tablespoons catsup
2 tablespoons lemon juice

Combine all ingredients in medium-size saucepan. Heat to boiling, stirring constantly, then simmer uncovered, stirring often, 15 minutes, or until thickened.

GOURMET STUFFED CHICKEN

White meat with a chicken liver stuffing, topped with crumbs and a dollop of gravy — serve this one to visiting celebrities, or maybe your in-laws.

Bake at 350° for 1 hour.
Makes 6 servings.

3 whole chicken breasts (about 2¹/₂ pounds)
2 cups Gourmet Stuffing
4 tablespoons (¹/₂ stick) butter or margarine
¹/₂ cup packaged cornflake crumbs
1 can (2 to a package) or 1 envelope mushroom soup mix

1. Halve breasts this way: Pull off skin, then cut along breastbone on either side, loosening meat as you go along, until each side can be pulled away in one piece. Snip out small bones. Pull each half breast open in the middle to form a pocket for stuffing. (Meat will come apart easily between its two large muscles.)
2. Make Gourmet Stuffing. Spoon into breast pockets to fill; press edges together and fasten with wooden picks.
3. Melt butter and margarine in large shallow baking pan; roll chicken in butter to coat well; arrange in single layer in same pan. Sprinkle crumbs over top.
4. Bake in moderate oven (350°) 1 hour, or until chicken is tender and golden.
5. Prepare mushroom soup mix, following label directions for gravy or sauce.
6. Place chicken on heated serving platter; remove wooden picks. Pass gravy in separate bowl to spoon over chicken.

GOURMET STUFFING

Makes 2 cups.

3 chicken livers
4 tablespoons (¹/₂ stick) butter or margarine
2 cups soft bread crumbs (4 slices)
2 tablespoons chopped onion
1 tablespoon water
1 teaspoon Worcestershire sauce
¹/₂ teaspoon salt

1. Sauté chicken livers in butter or margarine, stirring often, in small frying pan 5 minutes, or until livers lose their pink color.
2. Remove livers and chop, then add to bread crumbs in medium-sized bowl. Sauté onion just until soft in same frying pan.
3. Stir water, Worcestershire sauce, and salt into onions in frying pan; pour over crumb mixture. Toss lightly to mix well. (Mixture will be crumbly, not wet.)

CHAFING-DISH CHICKEN ROYALE

Perfect for a company buffet. Shrimps and tiny meat balls add the royal touches.

Makes 6 servings.

3 chicken breasts (about 12 ounces each), halved
4 cups water
Few celery tops
2¹/₂ teaspoons salt
¹/₂ pound meat-loaf mixture (ground beef and pork)
6 tablespoons flour
Dash of pepper
1 egg
2 teaspoons grated onion
¹/₄ cup milk
3 medium-size carrots, pared and sliced
1 cup frozen peas (from a 1¹/₄ pound bag)
4 tablespoons (¹/₂ stick) butter or margarine
1 tablespoon lemon juice
Few drops red-pepper seasoning
1 can (about 5 ounces) deveined shrimp, drained and rinsed
2 tablespoons chopped parsley

1. Combine chicken breasts, water, celery tops, and 2 teaspoons of the salt in a large saucepan; cover. Simmer 30 minutes, or until chicken is tender.
2. Remove from broth and cool until easy to handle. Pull off skin and take meat from bones in one piece; set aside for Step 7. Set broth aside for Step 4.
3. Combine meat-loaf mixture, 2 tablespoons of the flour, remaining ¹/₂ teaspoon salt, pepper, egg, onion, and milk in a medium-size bowl; mix with a fork until well-blended. Shape into 18 small balls. (Set remaining flour aside for making sauce).
4. Reheat chicken broth to boiling; add meat balls; cover. Poach 10 minutes or until cooked through; lift out with a slotted spoon and place in a bowl.
5. Cook carrots, covered, in part of the same chicken broth 20 minutes, or until tender; cook peas in remaining broth, following label directions. Drain liquid from each and strain into a 4-cup measure; add more water if needed, to make 4 cups. Keep carrots and peas hot for Step 7.
6. Melt butter or margarine in a large saucepan; blend in remaining 4 tablespoons flour; cook, stirring constantly, just until bubbly. Stir in the 4 cups chicken broth; continue cooking and stirring until sauce thickens and boils 1 minute. Stir in lemon juice and red-pepper seasoning.
7. Cut each half chicken breast into three pieces; add to sauce with meat balls, carrots, and peas. Heat slowly just to boiling; spoon into a chafing dish or heated serving dish. Arrange shrimps on top; sprinkle with parsley.

MOLDED CHICKEN INDIENNE

All white meat blends with curry and chutney for this inviting company-supper mold.

Makes 6 servings.

2 whole chicken breasts (about 12 ounces each)
3½ cups water
2 teaspoons salt
1 teaspoon curry powder
Few celery tops
2 envelopes unflavored gelatin
1 tablespoon sugar
2 tablespoons lemon juice
⅓ cup chutney (from a 6-ounce bottle), finely chopped
1 cup chopped celery

1. Combine chicken breasts with water, salt, curry powder, and celery tops in a large saucepan; cover; simmer 30 minutes, or until tender.
2. Remove chicken from broth; cool until easy to handle. Strain broth into a 4-cup measure; add water, if needed, to make 3½ cups. Pull skin from chicken and take meat from bones; chill meat; dice.
3. Soften gelatin with sugar in 1 cup of the broth in a medium-size saucepan; heat, stirring constantly, just until gelatin dissolves; remove from heat. Stir in remaining 2½ cups broth.
4. Measure ½ cup of the gelatin mixture into a small bowl; set aside for next step. Stir lemon juice into remaining gelatin in saucepan. Chill about 50 minutes, or until as thick as unbeaten egg white.
5. Stir chutney into gelatin in small bowl; pour into a 6-cup mold; chill about 30 minutes, or just until sticky-firm.
6. Fold chicken and celery into thickened gelatin in saucepan; spoon over sticky-firm chutney layer in mold. Chill overnight, or several hours until firm.
7. To unmold, run a sharp-tip thin-blade knife around top of mold, then dip very quickly in and out of a pan of hot water. Cover mold with serving plate; turn upside down; gently lift off mold. Garnish with leaves of Belgian endive, halved seedless grapes, and flaked coconut.

Quick and Easy   # CHICKEN CORDON BLEU

A party aristocrat, and easy to make in spite of its fancy French name.
Bake at 400° for 40 minutes.
Makes 4 servings.

2 whole chicken breasts (about 12 ounces each)
4 thin slices boiled ham, about 3 inches square
2 triangles (1 ounce each) process Gruyere cheese, sliced
4 tablespoons (½ stick) butter or margarine
½ cup fine dry bread crumbs
½ teaspoon salt
⅛ teaspoon paprika

1. Halve chicken breasts; remove skin, if you wish, then cut meat in one piece from bones. Pull each half breast open in the middle to make a deep pocket.
2. Fold ham around cheese slices, dividing evenly; tuck one into each pocket.
3. Melt butter or margarine in a pie plate; mix bread crumbs, salt, and paprika in a second pie plate.
4. Roll stuffed chicken breasts first in butter or margarine, then in crumb mixture to coat well. Place in a single layer in buttered baking dish.
5. Bake in hot oven (400°) 40 minutes, or until chicken is golden brown.

BAKED CHICKEN WITH WINE

Better not count on any leftovers when you serve this gourmet delight.

Bake at 350° about 1 hour.

Makes 4 servings.

1 broiler-fryer (2$^1/_2$ to 3 pounds), cut up
  in serving-size pieces
$^1/_4$ cup butter, margarine, or oil
1 medium-size onion, chopped ($^1/_2$ cup)
$^1/_2$ pound sliced fresh mushrooms OR
  1 can (3 to 4 ounces) sliced
  mushrooms, drained
1 can (10 ounces) condensed cream of
  mushroom soup, undiluted
$^3/_4$ cup dry sherry
1 tablespoon chopped parsley
1 teaspoon salt
1 teaspoon paprika
Dash pepper
1 or 2 lemon slices

1. Brown chicken slowly in butter, margarine, or oil. Remove from skillet and place in single layer in an 11x7-inch shallow baking dish.
2. Add mushrooms and onions to butter remaining in skillet and cook until tender, but not brown.
3. Add soup, sherry, seasonings, and lemon slices; blend thoroughly; pour over chicken.
4. Bake, uncovered, in moderate (350°) oven about 1 hour, or until chicken is fork-tender.

GULF COAST CHICKEN

From the bayou country: chicken, shrimp, and ham, in Spanish rice.

Bake at 350° for 30 minutes.

Makes 6 to 8 servings.

4 chicken legs (drumsticks and thighs)
2 tablespoons flour
1 teaspoon salt
$^1/_8$ teaspoon pepper
$^1/_4$ cup salad oil
2 packages Spanish rice mix
1 cup (8 ounces) diced smoked ham or
  cooked sausage
1 package (5 ounces) frozen cooked
  deveined shrimp, thawed
2 tablespoons instant chicken bouillon
4 cups hot water

1. Cut chicken legs into drumsticks and thighs; shake in paper bag with flour, salt, and pepper to coat evenly.
2. Sauté slowly in salad oil in large frying pan 30 minutes, or until fork-tender; place in 10-cup casserole with tight-fitting cover.
3. Sprinkle Spanish rice right from package over chicken; top with sliced meats, then shrimp.
4. Heat chicken bouillon and water to boiling in same frying pan, stirring until bouillon is dissolved; pour over mixture in casserole; cover.
5. Bake in moderate oven (350°) 30 minutes, or until bubbly-hot.

ORANGE GLAZED CHICKENS

This one is a showpiece: two glistening roasters, plumped with apricot stuffing.

Roast at 350° for 2 hours.
Makes 8 servings.

2 roasting chickens (about 4 pounds each)
Apricot-Walnut Stuffing
3 tablespoons butter or margarine, melted
Double Orange Glaze

1. Rinse chickens inside and out with cold water, drain, then pat dry.
2. Make Apricot Stuffing: pack lightly into neck and body cavities. Smooth neck skin over stuffing and skewer to back; twist wing tips flat against skewered neck skin; tie legs to tails with string. Place chickens on a rack in a roasting pan; brush with melted butter or margarine.
3. Roast in moderate oven (350°), basting several times with drippings in pan, 1¾ hours, or until chickens are almost tender.
4. While chickens cook, make Double Orange Glaze; brush part over each to coat generously.
5. Continue roasting, brushing twice with remaining glaze, 15 minutes, or until drumsticks move easily and chickens are richly glazed.
6. Remove to a heated large serving platter; take out skewers and cut away strings. Garnish platter with dried apricot halves topped with canned mandarin-orange seg-

ments, if you wish. Carve chickens into serving-size pieces.

DOUBLE ORANGE GLAZE: Combine ½ cup thawed frozen concentrated orange juice (from a 6-ounce can), ¼ cup orange marmalade, and 2 tablespoons bottled meat sauce in a small saucepan. Heat slowly, stirring constantly until marmalade melts and mixture is blended; remove from heat. Makes enough to glaze two 4-pound chickens.

APRICOT-WALNUT STUFFING

Makes 4 cups, or enough to stuff two 4-pound chickens.

1 medium-size onion, chopped (¹/₂ cup)
4 tablespoons (¹/₂ stick) butter or
** margarine**
¹/₂ cup chopped dried apricots
1 envelope instant chicken broth OR
** 1 chicken bouillon cube**
¹/₃ cup water
6 slices white bread, cubed (about 3 cups)
¹/₂ cup chopped walnuts

1. In a large frying pan, sauté onion in butter or margarine until soft; stir in apricots, chicken broth or bouillon cube, and water. Heat to boiling, crushing bouillon cube if used; remove from heat.
2. Add cubed bread and walnuts; toss until evenly moist.

Herb-Fried Drumsticks

CHICKEN FOR A CROWD

If you love to entertain, you are probably always on the lookout for wonderful recipes to feed a whole gaggle of guests. You especially want to make dishes that allow you to spend time with your company rather than labor in the kitchen during the party. The chicken recipes that follow should be able to rise to almost any occasion for you.

CHICKEN AND HAM SEVILLE

This impressive party dish can be made the day before: slices of chicken and stuffed rolls of ham bake with a spicy fruit glaze.

Bake at 350° about 1 hour.

Makes 12 servings.

6 whole chicken breasts, split
1 bottle (8 ounces) Italian salad dressing
2 tablespoons minced onion
1 cup diced celery
4 tablespoons (¹/₂ stick) butter or margarine
1¹/₄ cups water
1 can (6 ounces) frozen concentrated orange juice
1 package (8 ounces) ready-mix bread stuffing (4 cups)
¹/₄ cup chopped celery leaves
12 large slices boiled ham, cut not more than ¹/₈ inch thick (about 2 pounds)
¹/₂ cup orange marmalade
2 teaspoons ground ginger

1. Remove skin and snip off small rib bones from chicken breasts. Arrange in a single layer in large shallow baking pan, 13x9x2; pour salad dressing over; turn to coat all sides; cover lightly; let stand at room temperature, turning occasionally, 2 to 3 hours, or overnight in refrigerator.

2. Sauté onion and celery in butter or margarine 2 to 3 minutes in medium-size frying pan. Stir in water and ¹/₄ cup concentrated orange juice (save remaining ¹/₂ cup for Step 4); heat to boiling. Pour over bread stuffing and celery leaves in a large bowl; stir to moisten well.

3. Spoon a scant ¹/₂ cup stuffing into each slice of ham; roll up; fasten with a wooden pick if needed; place, folded side down, in single layer in greased large baking pan; cover lightly. (This much can be done a day ahead and kept chilled.)

4. About 1 hour before serving, take chicken and ham rolls from refrigerator. Drain marinade off chicken into a small bowl; stir in saved concentrated orange juice, marmalade, and ginger. Brush over chicken and ham.

5. Place chicken, uncovered, in moderate oven (350°). Bake, basting often with marmalade mixture, about 1 hour, or until tender and richly glazed.

6. Bake ham, uncovered, in same oven, also basting with marmalade mixture, about 40 minutes, or until heated through and glazed.

7. Arrange meats in separate piles on a heated platter; garnish with water cress and preserved kumquats stuck with fancy picks, if you wish.

OUTDOOR CHICKEN PARTY TIME

Allow plenty of grilling time so that the meat will almost fall off the bones.

Makes 12 servings.

- **6 broiler-fryers, split (1¹/₂ to 2 pounds each)**
- **2 cups salad oil**
- **¹/₂ cup lime or lemon juice**
- **2 teaspoons salt**
- **¹/₄ cup honey**

1. Wash chicken halves, then dry. Mix salad oil, lime or lemon juice, and salt in a small saucepan; brush part over chickens. Place, skin side up, on grill about 6 inches above hot coals.

2. Grill, turning and brushing often with more sauce, 1 hour.

3. Stir honey into remaining sauce; brush over chickens. Continue grilling, turning often and brushing with remaining sauce, 15 minutes, or until golden-brown and joints move easily.

CHICKEN AND FRUIT HARMONY

For a summer party: an elegant melange of tender chicken and fruits tossed with a creamy curry dressing.

Makes 12 servings.

- **2 broiler-fryers (2¹/₂ to 3 pounds each)**
- **4 cups water**
- **2 teaspoons salt**
- **12 peppercorns**
- **Handful of celery tops**
- **2 carrots, scraped and sliced**
- **Creamy Boiled Dressing**
- **3 cups cantaloupe cubes**
- **2 cups halved green grapes (about 1 pound)**
- **2 cups thinly sliced celery**
- **1 cup slivered almonds, toasted**
- **2 heads of Boston or leaf lettuce**
- **Paprika**

1. Simmer broiler-fryers in water with salt, peppercorns, celery tops, and carrots in large saucepan, covered, 45 minutes, or until tender.

2. Remove from broth and let cool just until easy to handle. (Save broth for soup for another meal.) Slip skin from chickens; remove meat from bones in large chunks and cut into cubes. (You should have about 6 cups.)

3. Place chicken in large bowl; toss with just enough Creamy Boiled Dressing to coat well; cover; chill.

4. When ready to serve, stir cantaloupe, grapes, celery, and almonds into chicken mixture; toss with enough of remaining dressing to coat well.

5. Line a salad bowl with lettuce; spoon salad in center; garnish with paprika.

CREAMY BOILED DRESSING

Makes 1½ cups.

- **4 tablespoons sugar**
- **2 tablespoons flour**
- **1 teaspoon salt**
- **¹/₂ teaspoon curry powder**
- **2 eggs, beaten**
- **1 cup water**
- **¹/₂ cup cider vinegar**
- **2 tablespoons butter or margarine**

1. Combine sugar, flour, salt, and curry powder in small saucepan; stir in egg, water, and vinegar.

2. Cook slowly, stirring constantly, 5 minutes, or until thickened. Remove from heat; stir in butter or margarine until melted. This dressing will keep well in a tightly covered jar in the refrigerator.

HERB-FRIED DRUMSTICKS

Quick and Easy

Everybody will love these, served informally, hot or cold.

Makes 12 to 18 servings.

36 chicken drumsticks
4 teaspoons salt
3 cups flour
2 teaspoons paprika
2 teaspoons dried thyme or tarragon
1½ cups buttermilk
Corn oil

1. Sprinkle drumsticks with 2 teaspoons of the salt. Combine flour with remaining salt, paprika, and thyme or tarragon.
2. Dip chicken in buttermilk; then roll in seasoned flour. Heat corn oil ½ inch deep in skillet; place drumsticks in hot oil.
3. Cook, uncovered, 15 to 20 minutes on each side, turning only once. Drain well on paper toweling.

Note: Milk may be substituted for buttermilk (decrease flour to 2 cups), but buttermilk is thicker and holds more flour to make a firmer coating.

PAELLA

From sunny Valencia comes this famous Spanish dish (pronounced pah-ay-ya). Made with chicken, shellfish, spicy sausages, and rice, it arrives at the table right in its pan, steaming hot.

Bake at 375° about 1 hour.
Makes 8 to 10 servings.

1 broiler-fryer, cut up
1 clove garlic, minced
¼ cup olive oil or salad oil
6 strands saffron
1½ cups raw long-grain rice
1 pound sweet Italian sausages, sliced 1 inch thick
1 large onion, chopped (1 cup)
1 green pepper, chopped
1 can (about 14 ounces) chicken broth
2 cans (about 7 ounces each) minced clams
1 teaspoon salt
1 teaspoon paprika
1 pound raw shrimps, shelled and deveined
4 tomatoes, sliced
1 pound fresh peas, shelled
1 can (4 ounces) pimientos, diced

1. Brown chicken with garlic in olive oil or salad oil in large frying pan; remove; stir in saffron and rice; sauté until rice is golden; add sausages, onion, and green pepper; sauté 7 to 10 minutes longer; stir in chicken broth, minced clams and their liquid, salt, and paprika; cover, and cook 10 minutes.
2. Layer chicken, rice mixture, shrimps, tomatoes, peas, and pimientos in a 12-cup baking dish; cover tightly. (Or use a metal paella pan.)
3. Bake in moderate oven (375°) 1 hour, or until rice is tender and liquid is absorbed.
4. Remove cover; garnish paella with more diced pimientos and a few freshly steamed clams in their shells, if you wish.
5. Serve from its baking dish at the table with thick slices of crusty bread and a big green salad; add fresh fruit and coffee for dessert, or in true Spanish style serve a chilled creamy baked caramel custard.

JAMBALAYA

2 broiler-fryers (about 2 pounds each), cut up
3 cups diced cooked ham (1 pound)
4 tablespoons (½ stick) butter or margarine
2 cloves garlic, sliced
3 large onions, chopped (3 cups)
1 package (1 pound) frozen deveined shelled raw shrimps
3 cans (about 1 pound each) stewed tomatoes
2 teaspoons salt
¼ teaspoon liquid red-pepper seasoning
1 large bay leaf
3 cups thinly sliced celery
2 cups uncooked rice
¼ cup chopped parsley

A kettle of contrasts from Creole country: Chicken, ham, vegetables, rice.
Makes 12 servings.

1. Wash chicken pieces; pat dry.
2. Brown ham lightly in butter or margarine in a heavy roasting pan. Stir in garlic and onions; sauté 5 minutes, or until soft. Add chicken and shrimps.
3. Combine tomatoes, salt, red-pepper seasoning, and bay leaf in a large bowl; pour over ham and chicken.
4. Heat to boiling; cover. Simmer 30 minutes. Stir in celery and rice, making sure all rice is covered with liquid.
5. Simmer 30 minutes longer, or until chicken and rice are tender; remove bay leaf. Stir in parsley.

CHICKEN AND HAM BURGOO

A meal to come home for: robust stew, perfect for an after-the-game or after-skating crowd of hungry dynamos.

Makes 12 servings.

1 roasting chicken (about 3 pounds)
4 smoked ham hocks, (about 1 pound each)
Water
3 teaspoons salt
½ teaspoon cayenne pepper
2 cups diced pared potatoes
2 cups diced pared carrots
2 large onions, chopped (2 cups)
1 package (10 ounces) frozen Fordhook lima beans
2 cups shredded cabbage
2 cups fresh corn kernels
2 cups thinly sliced celery
2 cups diced tomatoes
1 package (10 ounces) frozen whole okra
2 tablespoons Worcestershire sauce
1 cup diced green pepper
½ cup chopped parsley

1. Combine chicken and ham hocks in a kettle or roasting pan; add just enough water to cover. Heat to boiling; cover. Simmer 1½ hours, or until chicken is tender; remove from kettle. Continue cooking ham hocks 1 hour, or until tender; remove from kettle.
2. Let broth stand until fat rises to top, then skim off. Measure broth and return 12 cups to kettle. Stir in salt, cayenne, potatoes, carrots, onions, and lima beans. Heat to boiling; simmer 15 minutes.
3. While vegetables cook, remove skin from chicken and ham hocks; take meat from bones, discarding fat; dice meat.
4. Stir cabbage, corn, celery, tomatoes, okra, and Worcestershire sauce into kettle; simmer 15 minutes, or until all vegetables are crisply tender. Stir in green pepper, parsley, and diced meats; heat just to boiling.
5. Ladle into soup plates or bowls. Serve with corn bread or crusty hard rolls, if you wish.

CLUB NIGHT CASSEROLE

This agreeable casserole will please all comers. It's best started the day before.

Bake at 350° for 50 to 60 minutes.
Makes 8 to 12 servings.

1 stewing chicken (about 5 pounds),
   not cut up
3¹/₂ cups water
1 medium-size onion, sliced
1 carrot, scraped and halved
Handful of celery tops
2 teaspoons salt
1 bay leaf
6 cups cooked rice (1¹/₂ cups raw)
6 tablespoons chicken fat
6 tablespoons flour
1 cup light or table cream
2 cans (3 or 4 ounces each) sliced
   mushrooms
1 can (about 4 ounces) pimientos, diced
1 cup (about a 5-ounce can) toasted
   slivered almonds
1 cup buttered soft bread crumbs (2 slices)

1. Combine chicken, water, onion, carrot, celery tops, salt, and bay leaf in large kettle; cover; simmer 1 to 1½ hours, or until tender.
2. Cool chicken in stock; remove, and skin. Take meat from bones; cut meat into bite-size pieces; place in medium-size bowl. Pour ½ cup stock over to keep chicken moist; cover and chill.
3. Strain remaining stock into a medium-size bowl; chill; skim off fat and save for Step 5. (This much can be done the day before.)
4. When ready to complete dish, heat 1 cup stock and pour over cooked rice in large bowl; let stand while making sauce.
5. Melt chicken fat from Step 3 in medium-size saucepan, adding butter or margarine, if needed, to make 6 tablespoons. Remove from heat; blend in flour; stir in 2 cups stock.
6. Cook over low heat, stirring constantly, until sauce thickens and boils 1 minute. Remove from heat; gradually stir in cream, mushrooms and their liquid, pimientos, almonds, and chicken; season to taste with salt and pepper.
7. Make alternate layers of chicken and rice mixtures in buttered 12-cup casserole; sprinkle buttered bread crumbs around edge.
8. Bake in moderate oven (350°) 50 to 60 minutes, or until sauce bubbles around edges and crumbs are golden-brown.

Lone Ranger Chicken

CHICKEN FOR ONE

Happy is the man who doesn't have to fix his own supper on the nights when his wife's work schedule — or classes, or committee meetings — keep her away at the dinner hour. For couples in this situation (or for anyone who cooks for solo meals), here are six chicken recipes that can be prepared ahead and left waiting for a few hours in oven or refrigerator, or prepared in two separate portions for two days' single eating. They should make a loner's dinner — or lunch — a more pleasant affair.

LONER'S SALAMI-CHICKEN DUO

These spicy drumsticks taste delicious hot or cold.

Makes 1 serving for 2 meals.

2 chicken drumsticks with thighs
1 slice (1 ounce) salami
2 tablespoons flour
1/2 teaspoon salt
1/4 teaspoon paprika
1/4 teaspoon leaf oregano, crumbled
Dash pepper
3 tablespoons vegetable oil

1. Cut through chicken legs at joints to separate drumsticks and thighs, then cut an opening along bone of each drumstick and in meaty part of each thigh with a sharp knife to make a pocket for stuffing.
2. Cut salami into 4 strips; stuff 1 strip into each piece of chicken.
3. Shake pieces, a few at a time, in mixture of flour, salt, paprika, oregano, and pepper in a bag to coat evenly.
4. Cook pieces slowly in vegetable oil in a medium-size frying pan 20 minutes; turn; cover loosely. Cook 20 minutes longer, or until tender and crisply golden. Remove from pan and drain on paper towel. Wrap tightly in foil and place in oven or refrigerator to keep.

BIRD SOLITAIRE

This delicious piece of chicken will wait in the refrigerator until you (or your husband) are ready to bake it for supper.

1 chicken leg with thigh, OR 1 large
chicken breast (about 12 ounces)
2 tablespoons buttermilk
2 tablespoons packaged corn-flake crumbs
2 tablespoons flour
1/4 teaspoon salt
1/4 teaspoon poultry seasoning
1 tablespoon melted butter or margarine

Bake at 425° about 45 minutes.

Makes 1 serving.

1. Remove chicken skin, if you wish, then sprinkle buttermilk on both sides of chicken piece; coat with mixture of corn-flake crumbs, flour, salt, and poultry seasoning; arrange chicken piece in small well-buttered baking pan; pour melted butter or margarine over. Refrigerate.
2. Bake in hot oven (425°) 45 minutes, or until tender.

BOWLING-NIGHT SALAD

Stash these cooling little salads in the refrigerator for someone's dinner tonight — and tomorrow night.

Makes 3 individual molds.

1 broiler-fryer (about 2¹/₂ pounds), cut up
3 cups water
¹/₂ small onion, sliced
Few celery tops
1¹/₂ teaspoons salt
3 peppercorns
1 envelope unflavored gelatin
¹/₄ cup apple juice
¹/₂ cup mayonnaise or salad dressing
¹/₄ cup diced celery
2 tablespoons chopped toasted slivered almonds
2 tablespoons chopped stuffed green olives
Boston lettuce

1. Combine chicken, water, onion, celery tops, salt, and peppercorns in a kettle; cover. Simmer 1 hour, or until chicken is very tender; remove from broth. Strain broth into a 2-cup measure.
2. Soften gelatin in apple juice in a medium-size saucepan; stir in 1½ cups of the broth. (Chill any remaining broth to add to soup for another meal.)
3. Heat gelatin mixture slowly, stirring constantly, until gelatin dissolves; remove from heat. Cool for Step 5.
4. Pull skin from chicken and take meat from bones; dice fine. (There should be about 2 cups.)
5. Blend mayonnaise or salad dressing into gelatin mixture in saucepan; pour into an ice-cube tray. Freeze 20 minutes, or until firm about 1 inch in from edges.
6. Spoon into a chilled large bowl; beat until fluffy thick. Fold in diced chicken, celery, almonds, and olives. Spoon into 3 individual molds. Chill several hours or until firm.
7. Salad can be eaten from the mold, or unmolded onto a lettuce-lined plate and garnished with melon crescents.

SUPERMARKET CHICKEN SUPPER

A ready-barbecued chicken and prepared macaroni salad from the supermarket can make 2 dinners for a loner.
Makes 1 serving for 2 meals.

1 container (1 pound) prepared macaroni salad
¹/₂ package (4 ounces) shredded Cheddar cheese
¹/₂ small can (7 to 8 ounces) lima beans, drained
¹/₄ cup chopped celery
¹/₄ teaspoon fines herbes
¹/₂ small head chicory, washed, dried, and separated into leaves
1 medium-size tomato, cut in wedges
1 ready-to-eat barbecued chicken (about 2 pounds)
Sweet mixed pickles
Stuffed green olives

1. Combine macaroni salad, cheese, lima beans, celery, and herbes in a large bowl; toss lightly to mix well. Chill at least an hour to season.
2. Line a platter with chicory leaves; break remaining into bite-size pieces in center; spoon half the macaroni salad on top. Tuck tomato wedges around salad. Put rest of salad in a covered refrigerator container for next meal.
3. Cut chicken in half with kitchen scissors; place one half, skin side up, on platter beside salad. Wrap other half in transparent wrap and place in meat keeper compartment of refrigerator for tomorrow's meal.
4. Garnish with pickles and olives, and serve with rye bread-and-butter sandwiches, if you wish.

LONE RANGER CHICKEN

The sauce will help keep this chicken from drying out — either in the oven or the refrigerator — until it's needed for a single dinner.

Bake at 400° about 1 hour.

Makes 1 serving for 2 meals.

2 large chicken breasts OR 2 legs with
 thighs
Butter or margarine
Savory Sauce

1. Wash chicken pieces; pat dry; remove skin if you wish.
2. Arrange chicken pieces in a single layer in a well-buttered shallow baking pan.
3. Spoon Savory Sauce over so chicken pieces are well coated.
4. Bake, uncovered, in hot oven (400°) about 1 hour, or until chicken is tender.
5. Remove one breast or leg with half the sauce, and cool; then refrigerate in a covered jar for reheating tomorrow (or perhaps the next day, but better not keep it longer than that).
6. Leave other breast or leg tightly covered in the oven (with the heat off) to be eaten within an hour or two, or refrigerate in a small covered baking dish for reheating the same night.

SAVORY SAUCE

Makes 1½ cups.

1 can (8 ounces) tomato sauce
1 small onion, chopped
½ teaspoon garlic powder
2 tablespoons soy sauce
1 tablespoon sugar
½ teaspoon dry mustard
Dash cayenne pepper

Mix all ingredients in a medium-size bowl.

SINGLE SAM'S SALAD SANDWICH

Delicious chicken salad makes 2 summer suppers (or 1 for a hungry husband).

Makes 1 serving for 1 or 2 meals.

1 whole chicken breast (about 12 ounces),
 OR 1 can (5 or 6 ounces) boned chicken,
 diced
1 cup water
1 small onion, sliced
Handful of celery tops
½ plus ¼ teaspoon salt
Pepper
½ cup diced celery
¼ cup slivered almonds
4 tablespoons mayonnaise
1 tablespoon milk
⅛ teaspoon dry mustard
1 or 2 large Vienna rolls
Lettuce
Cherry tomatoes

1. If using chicken breast, place it in a medium-size saucepan with water, onion, celery tops, ½ teaspoon salt, and a dash of pepper. Simmer, covered, 20 to 30 minutes, or until chicken is tender. Let stand until cool enough to handle, then skin chicken and take meat from bones. Dice chicken (you should have about 1 cup).
2. Combine chicken, celery, and almonds in medium-size bowl. Mix mayonnaise, milk, ¼ teaspoon salt, mustard, and a dash of pepper; stir into chicken mixture, tossing lightly to mix. If making 2 portions, chill 1 portion on a plate until serving time; place remainder in a covered refrigerator container in coldest part of refrigerator for tomorrow's meal.
3. At mealtime, split Vienna roll and butter it. Line buttered roll with lettuce; fill with salad. Garnish with cherry tomatoes.

Mexicali Chicken

CHICKEN SOUTH-OF-THE-BORDER

Latin-American cuisine reflects the influences of the many nations that have occupied the lands and islands south of the United States. It also reflects the ways of the original settlers — the Indians — in their use of native fruits, vegetables, and spices. The result is richly varied food, a sampling of which you will find here: several chicken dishes from Mexico, an Argentine chicken-in-sherry, a few delectable examples of Caribbean chicken.

MEXICALI CHICKEN

Chicken and peppers are steeped in a tangy tomato sauce — cook this in your gayest casserole.

Bake at 350° for 1½ hours.
Makes 8 servings.

2 broiler-fryers (about 3 pounds each), cut up
2 tablespoons butter or margarine
2 tablespoons olive oil or vegetable oil
1 large onion, chopped (1 cup)
1 large sweet green pepper, quartered, seeded, and chopped
1 large sweet red pepper, quartered, seeded, and chopped
3 teaspoons chili powder
¼ cup flour
1 can (about 2 pounds) Italian tomatoes
3 teaspoons salt
1 teaspoon sugar
¼ teaspoon pepper

1. Wash chicken pieces and dry. Brown, part at a time, in butter or margarine and olive oil or vegetable oil in a large frying pan; remove all from pan and set aside while making the sauce.
2. Stir onion and green and red peppers into drippings in pan; sauté until soft. Stir in chili powder; cook 1 minute longer.
3. Sprinkle flour over top, then blend in; stir in tomatoes, salt, sugar, and pepper. Cook, stirring constantly, until sauce thickens and boils 1 minute.
4. Layer browned chicken, topping each with part of the sauce, into a 12-cup baking dish; cover.
5. Bake in moderate oven (350°) 1 hour; uncover. Bake 30 minutes longer, or until chicken is tender and sauce is thickened slightly. Garnish with rings of red and green pepper, if you wish.

CHICKEN VERACRUZ

Serve this dish to guests with adventure-some palates — the sauce is a hot one, heady with spices and tart with orange.

Makes 6 servings.

3 chicken breasts (about 12 ounces each)
3 tablespoons butter or margarine
1 tablespoon peanut oil or salad oil
$\frac{1}{2}$ teaspoon salt
Pepper
$\frac{1}{3}$ cup brandy
2 cloves garlic, thinly sliced
Small can (about 4 ounces) peeled green
  chilis, chopped
Few drops red-pepper seasoning
1 can (6 ounces) frozen orange juice
  concentrate, undiluted
$\frac{1}{2}$ cup pine nuts
$\frac{1}{2}$ red pepper, thinly sliced, and orange
  slices (for garnish)

1. Halve chicken breasts.
2. Heat butter or margarine and the oil in a skillet and sauté chicken breasts until golden. Season with salt and a few dashes of pepper, pour brandy over and set aflame. (Flaming burns off the alcohol but leaves a delicious taste.)
3. When flames have died down, add garlic, chilis, and red-pepper seasoning. Blend in undiluted orange juice. Simmer 20 to 25 minutes, turning chicken breasts several times.
4. When chicken breasts are tender, remove to a hot platter and pour sauce over. Sprinkle with pine nuts. Garnish with pepper and orange slices.

PORT ANTONIO PULLET

A spicy, authentic Jamaican dish as prepared by the Jamaica Arms restaurant in New York.

Roast at 325° for 1½ hours.
Makes 4 servings.

1 broiler-fryer (about 3 pounds)
2 cloves garlic
1 teaspoon ground ginger (the Jamaica
  Arms recommends fresh ginger root, if
  you can get it; if so, use 3 teaspoons root
  pieces)
$\frac{1}{2}$ teaspoon paprika
$\frac{1}{2}$ teaspoon salt
$\frac{1}{2}$ teaspoon pepper
Juice of 1 lime
2 tablespoons olive oil
$\frac{1}{4}$ cup dry sherry
Paprika-and-Olive Sauce

1. Wash chicken, pat dry. Rub cavity with 1 garlic clove, and half of the ginger, paprika, salt, pepper, and lime juice.
2. Tie chicken legs and rub skin with remaining garlic clove, plus remaining ginger, paprika, salt, pepper, and lime juice mixed with 1 tablespoon of the oil.
3. Roast at 325° for 1½ hours, basting twice with drippings plus the sherry and the remaining oil.
4. When chicken is done, remove to a hot platter and prepare Paprika-and-Olive Sauce in the pan the chicken cooked in.
5. Pour sauce over chicken, garnish with lime wedges, serve with black-eyed peas.

PAPRIKA-AND-OLIVE SAUCE: Put roasting pan over a medium flame and stir 2 teaspoons flour into the pan drippings. Add ½ cup water, ¼ cup dry sherry, ¼ cup heavy cream, 1 teaspoon paprika, ½ teaspoon salt, ¼ teaspoon pepper, and about 12 green olives. Simmer until thickened.

ARROZ CON POLLO CRIOLLO

This Cuban-style chicken with saffron rice is colorful, fragrant, flavorsome.

Bake at 375° for 1¼ hours.

Makes 6 servings.

2 broiler-fryers (about 2½ pounds each), cut in serving-size pieces
3 teaspoons salt
¼ cup olive oil or vegetable oil
1 medium-size onion, chopped (½ cup)
1 small green pepper, halved, seeded, and chopped
2 cloves garlic, minced
1 can (8 ounces) tomato sauce
1 cup dry white wine
2½ cups water
½ teaspoon ground cumin
½ teaspoon pepper
½ teaspoon leaf oregano, crumbled
Few strands saffron, crushed
¼ teaspoon paprika
1½ cups uncooked rice
1 package (10 ounces) frozen green peas
1 pimiento, chopped

1. Sprinkle chicken with 1 teaspoon of the salt. Brown, part at a time, in olive oil in a large frying pan; remove and set aside.
2. Stir onion, green pepper, and garlic into drippings in frying pan; sauté until soft. Stir in tomato sauce, wine, water, remaining 2 teaspoons salt, cumin, pepper, oregano, saffron, paprika, and rice; heat to boiling. Pour into a 12-cup baking dish; arrange chicken on top; cover.
3. Bake in moderate oven (375°) 1 hour and 15 minutes, or until chicken and rice are tender and liquid is absorbed.
4. While chicken cooks, cook peas, following label directions; drain. Spoon around edge of baking dish; garnish with pimiento.

POLLO CON PASAS

A lovely dish from Mexico that includes raisins (the "pasas") and olives.

Makes 6 to 8 servings.

2 broiler-fryers (2½ to 3 pounds each), cut in serving-size pieces
¼ cup all-purpose flour
5 tablespoons butter or margarine
1 medium-size onion, thinly sliced
2 large tomatoes, chopped
½ cup pimiento-stuffed olives, sliced
1 cup seedless raisins
1½ teaspoons salt
¼ teaspoon pepper
¼ teaspoon chili powder
½ teaspoon sugar
2 cups cold water
Green pepper slices

1. Dust chicken pieces with flour. Heat butter or margarine in a large skillet and fry chicken until golden brown on both sides.
2. Remove chicken, set aside. Sauté onions in same skillet until transparent. Add tomatoes, then replace chicken. Add sliced olives, raisins, salt, pepper, chili powder, sugar, and water.
3. Heat to boiling; reduce heat and simmer, covered, 45 minutes or until chicken is fork-tender.
4. Arrange chicken on heated platter, pour sauce over, and serve hot, garnished with green pepper slices.

TOBAGO CHICKEN-AVOCADO SOUP

An elegant hot soup to precede a luncheon or supper party or special occasion dinner.

Makes 4 to 6 servings.

2¹/₂ tablespoons flour
3 tablespoons melted butter or margarine
¹/₃ cup heavy cream (whipping cream)
2¹/₂ cups chicken broth (canned or saved)
2 tablespoons finely minced green pepper
1 cup chopped, peeled avocado
¹/₂ teaspoon salt
¹/₈ teaspoon dried basil
Lemon slices

1. Stir flour into melted butter or margarine in saucepan. Add cream, 1½ cups of the chicken broth, and minced green pepper. Stir over medium flame until boiling. Reduce heat and simmer 3 minutes.
2. In blender, or with rotary beater, blend chopped peeled avocado with remaining 1 cup chicken broth until smooth. Add to pan with the salt; heat through; add the basil. Serve hot with the lemon slices.

SAN ANGEL POLLO RANCHERO

Ranch-house chicken, Mexican-style, is not plain or rustic but spicy and sophisticated.

Roast at 375° for 1½ hours.
Makes 8 servings.

3 whole broiler-fryers (2¹/₂ to 3 pounds each)
3 to 4 cups dry white wine
3 cloves garlic, minced
2 teaspoons salt
1 teaspoon marjoram
1 teaspoon pepper
6 tablespoons melted lard or butter
Refried Beans

1. Mix wine, garlic, and seasonings and soak chicken in this marinade for 4 hours, turning frequently. Pat dry.
2. Brush chickens with melted lard or butter. Roast at 375° for 1½ hours, basting often with pan drippings.
3. Serve on Refried Beans.

REFRIED BEANS: Heat 6 tablespoons lard in a large heavy skillet. Add 1 minced onion and 1 minced garlic clove and cook until golden. Stir in 3 cups mashed, cooked kidney beans, 1 teaspoon salt, and ½ teaspoon pepper. Cook until dry. Makes 8 servings.

CHICKEN ARGENTINE

The cooking fragrance of this scrumptuous dish will whet the appetite of all withing sniffing distance.

Makes 4 servings.

1 broiler-fryer (about 3 pounds), cut in serving-size pieces
¹/₄ cup vegetable oil
2 teaspoons salt
¹/₂ teaspoon ground nutmeg
¹/₂ teaspoon garlic powder
¹/₄ teaspoon pepper
¹/₂ cup dry sherry

1. In a medium-size frying pan, brown chicken in vegetable oil, 10 minutes on each side.
2. Mix salt, nutmeg, garlic powder, and pepper in a cup; sprinkle over chicken; drizzle with sherry; cover pan.
3. Simmer 40 minutes, or until chicken is tender.

JAMAICA CHICKEN FEAST

Because of the pepper and allspice sprinkled on the bird, this recipe is sometimes called Freckled Chicken — a homely name for an elegant dish with a delicate and subtle flavor.

Roast at 450° for 15 minutes, then at 350° for about 45 minutes.

Makes 4 servings.

1 small roasting chicken (about 3¹/₂ pounds)
¹/₂ lime
1 or 2 bunches of parsley
2 garlic cloves, sliced in halves
¹/₄ cup melted butter or margarine
Allspice and pepper (Note: No salt is used because island chefs claim salt draws moisture from the chicken, leaving it dry and tasteless after cooking.)
Fresh parsley and cherry tomatoes for garnish
Jamaica-Style Pimiento Rice
Blue Mountain Angel's Food

1. Preheat oven to 450°. Rub cavity of chicken with lime. Stuff cavity full of parsley, placing garlic slivers up under the breasts. (The parsley will hold the garlic in place during cooking. The stuffing flavors the bird; it is not eaten.)
2. Brush chicken three times with melted butter or margarine, allowing each coat to dry. Sprinkle with grated allspice and pepper. (Allspice grows only in Jamaica; some cooks there add it to the parsley stuffing, as well as sprinkle it over the chicken.)
3. Place chicken on a rack in an open pan, sear for 15 minutes at 450°, reduce heat to 350° and roast for another ¾ hour, or until a drumstick moves easily at joint.
4. Put chicken on a hot platter and surround it with fresh parsley and cherry tomatoes. Serve with Jamaica-Style Pimiento Rice and Blue Mountain Angel's Food.

Note: You can barbecue this chicken rather than roast it, if you wish. Use a quartered instead of whole chicken, rub the quarters with lime, then pepper, and brush with oil before placing them on a grill. Cook, turning frequently, 1½ hours or until drumstick moves easily at joint.

JAMAICA-STYLE PIMIENTO RICE
¹/₂ onion, diced
¹/₂ green pepper, diced
1 clove garlic
4 tablespoons salad oil
1¹/₂ cups precooked packaged rice
1¹/₂ cups tomato juice
1 small can (4 ounces) pimientos, diced (reserve liquid)
1 teaspoon salt
Black pepper
1 can (6 ounces) mushrooms and their liquid, if desired
Diced green or black olives, if desired

1. Sauté onion, pepper, and garlic clove (mash it up) in oil in a large skillet until onion is transparent.
2. Add rice, tomato juice, pimientos and their liquid, salt, and a generous dash of pepper (or grind of a pepper mill).
3. Bring to boil, turn off heat, and let rice stand till all liquid is absorbed, about 5 minutes.
4. Fluff rice. Add mushrooms and their liquid, if desired, or garnish with olives. Serve hot.

BLUE MOUNTAIN ANGEL'S FOOD: The Jamaicans advise, "peel and peg your oranges," which is their colorful way of saying, "Cut oranges (one per person) into sections and arrange them in a dish, then sprinkle lavishly with freshly grated coconut."

Twin Chickens Parisienne

CONTINENTAL CHICKEN

One of the greatest pleasures of living in a world that grows smaller every day is that the wonderful food of other countries — their produce and their recipes — has become available to us. What better way to liven up the family's regular mealtime repertoire, or to add interest to company dinners, than by serving a chicken dish from the famous cuisine of France or Italy, of Spain, Hungary, or Russia? For additional chicken recipes with a Continental accent, see Stuffed Drumsticks Napoli in the DRUMSTICKS section, Chicken Livers Strogonoff in LIVERS, and the low-calorie Paella in CHICKEN ON A DIET.

COQ AU VIN

Chicken cooked in wine is a traditional French dish. This recipe calls for red wine, but white wine is often used also.

Makes 6 servings.

1 stewing chicken (about 4 pounds), cut in
   serving-size pieces
¼ cup flour
2 teaspoons salt
¼ teaspoon pepper
3 tablespoons butter or margarine
1 slice ham (about 8 ounces), diced
8 tiny white onions, diced
2 tablespoons finely chopped parsley
Pinch of thyme
1 clove garlic
1 cup dry red wine
1 can button mushrooms (6 to 8 ounces),
   drained

1. Wash chicken; drain. Shake pieces, a few at a time, in mixture of flour, salt, and pepper in a paper bag to coat well.
2. Heat butter or margarine in large heavy skillet and brown chicken.
3. Add diced ham, onions, parsley, and seasonings. Stir until all are slightly browned.
4. Add wine and lower heat. Cover skillet and simmer slowly 1½ hours, or until chicken is tender.
5. Add mushrooms and simmer another 15 minutes.
6. If you wish to thicken sauce, remove chicken to a hot platter and stir several *roux* into liquid in pan. (To make *roux*, heat a little butter in a small saucepan and stir in enough flour to enable you to form little balls of the mixture.)
7. Pour sauce over chicken on platter and serve hot.

TWIN CHICKENS PARISIENNE

Stuffed with parsley, simmered in mushroom sauce, the birds are then bathed in gravy and presented on a bed of noodles.

Makes 6 to 8 servings.

2 whole broiler-fryers (about 3 pounds each)
1 teaspoon salt
¹/₂ teaspoon sugar
2 bunches parsley, washed and trimmed
2 tablespoons butter or margarine
1 can (3 or 4 ounces) whole mushrooms
¹/₄ teaspoon pepper
2 tablespoons flour
³/₄ cup cream
Hot cooked noodles

1. Rinse chickens inside and out with cold water; drain, then pat dry. Sprinkle insides with ½ teaspoon of the salt and sugar; place parsley in body cavities, packing in lightly. Skewer neck skin to back; twist wing tips flat against skewered neck skin; tie the legs to tails with string.
2. Brown in butter or margarine in a heavy kettle or Dutch oven; turn breast side up.
3. Drain liquid from mushrooms into a 1-cup measure; add water to make ¾ cup; pour over chickens. Sprinkle with remaining ½ teaspoon salt and pepper; cover tightly. (Set mushrooms aside for Step 6.)
4. Simmer, basting several times with liquid in kettle, 1 hour and 15 minutes, or until tender. Remove from kettle and keep hot while making gravy.
5. Pour liquid from kettle into a 2-cup measure; let stand about a minute, or until fat rises to top, then skim off into a cup. Add water to liquid, if needed, to make 1 cup.
6. Measure 2 tablespoons of the fat and return to kettle; blend in flour; stir in the 1 cup liquid. Cook, stirring constantly, until gravy thickens and boils 1 minute. Stir in mushrooms and cream; heat slowly just to boiling. Darken with a few drops bottled gravy coloring, if you wish.
7. Spoon noodles into a heated large serving bowl. Take out skewers and cut strings from chickens; arrange chickens on top of noodles; spoon gravy over all. Garnish with parsley, if you wish. Carve chickens into serving-size pieces.

CHICKEN TARRAGON CHAMPIGNONS

A French dish of herb-flavored chicken and fresh mushrooms.

Makes 4 servings.

1 broiler-fryer (3 pounds), cut up in serving-size pieces
1 tablespoon seasoned salt
¹/₂ teaspoon fresh ground pepper
Dash of paprika
1 teaspoon tarragon
¹/₄ cup cooking oil OR ¹/₂ stick melted butter or margarine
1 medium onion, thinly sliced
¹/₂ pound fresh mushrooms, trimmed and sliced

1. Sprinkle chicken pieces with blended salt, pepper, and paprika.
2. Cook chicken slowly to a deep golden brown in the butter, margarine, or oil, 15 to 25 minutes, turning to brown all sides; remove chicken and keep hot.
3. In the skillet cook the onions and mushrooms until tender but not brown.
4. Return chicken to skillet, sprinkle with tarragon and cover chicken with the vegetables. Cover skillet and continue cooking, slowly, until thickest pieces are fork-tender, about 20 minutes.

CHICKEN PILAF PROVENCAL

This French peasant chicken-rice dish is for true garlic lovers.

Makes 6 servings.

2 broiler-fryers (about 2 pounds each), cut in serving-size pieces
4 tablespoons olive oil
2 tablespoons butter
1 tablespoon flour
2½ cups chicken broth
1 teaspoon salt
30 (well, all right, 20 then) garlic cloves, peeled
¾ cup long-grain rice

1. In a heavy kettle, brown chicken pieces thoroughly in 2 tablespoons olive oil and the butter. Remove chicken and set aside.
2. Stir in the flour, broth, salt, and garlic cloves. Bring to boil.
3. When sauce boils, return chicken to kettle and simmer, covered, 45 minutes.
4. Meanwhile, sauté rice in 2 tablespoons olive oil until opaque. When chicken has cooked 45 minutes, add rice, easing it down into the liquid with a fork. Simmer, covered, 20 minutes longer. Serve in the kettle it has cooked in.

CHICKEN TETRAZZINI

This excellent chicken-spaghetti-cheese dish is an all-time party favorite — especially with hostesses, who can make it ahead of time.

Bake at 425° for 20 minutes.

Makes 6 servings.

1 package (8 ounces) thin spaghetti
1 small onion, chopped (¼ cup)
2 tablespoons butter or margarine
2 tablespoons flour
1 envelope instant chicken broth OR
  1 chicken bouillon cube
1 teaspoon salt
1 teaspoon dry mustard
½ teaspoon pepper
1 large can evaporated milk
1 can (3 or 4 ounces) sliced mushrooms
2 pimientos, diced
3 cups diced cooked chicken
1 cup (¼ pound) grated sharp Cheddar cheese
¼ cup grated Parmesan cheese

1. Cook spaghetti, following label directions; drain; place in buttered 8-cup shallow baking dish.
2. While spaghetti cooks, sauté onion in butter or margarine until soft in large saucepan. Remove from heat; blend in flour, instant broth or bouillon cube, salt, dry mustard, and pepper. Slowly stir in evaporated milk, then liquid from mushrooms plus water to make 1½ cups. Cook, stirring constantly, until sauce thickens and boils 1 minute; stir in mushrooms and pimientos.
3. Mix 2 cups sauce with drained spaghetti in baking dish, making a well in center to hold the chicken mixture.
4. Combine chicken with remaining sauce; spoon into dish with spaghetti; sprinkle cheeses on top.
5. Bake in hot oven (450°) 20 minutes, or until bubbly and golden. (If made ahead, cover lightly, cool, then chill until 30 minutes before baking. If put into oven cold, allow an additional 15 to 20 minutes' baking time.)

CHICKEN RISOTTO

Inspired by a famous Italian dish, this recipe calls for toasted rice. The saffron gives it a lovely color.

Bake at 350° about 1½ hours.

Makes 6 servings.

1 cup raw long-grain rice
2 broiler-fryers (about 2 pounds each), cut up
3 tablespoons flour
4 tablespoons salad oil or olive oil
1 medium-size onion, chopped (½ cup)
1 clove garlic, minced
1 cup chopped celery
1 teaspoon salt
3 strands saffron, crushed
½ cup water
1 can condensed beef consomme
1 can (1 pound) cut green beans, drained
¼ cup toasted almonds
1 tablespoon chopped parsley

1. Spread rice in shallow metal baking pan, 13x9x2; toast in moderate oven (350°), stirring once or twice, 15 minutes, or until golden-brown; empty at once into strainer; rinse under cold running water; save for Step 3.

2. Remove skin from chicken pieces; snip out small bones from breasts. Shake chicken with flour in bag until well coated. Brown, a few pieces at a time, in salad oil or olive oil in large frying pan; remove and set aside.

3. Sauté onion and garlic in same frying pan; stir in rice, celery, salt, saffron, and water. Pour into 10-cup shallow baking dish; arrange chicken on top; pour consomme over; cover.

4. Bake in moderate oven (350°) 1 hour and 20 minutes, or until rice is popped and liquid absorbed. Spoon green beans over chicken in small mounds; cover; bake 10 minutes longer, or until beans are heated through.

5. Sprinkle top of casserole with almonds and parsley just before serving.

Quick and Easy

QUICK CACCIATORE

An easy way to make the Italian favorite.

Makes 4 servings

1 medium-size onion, chopped (½ cup)
3 tablespoons salad oil
1 broiler-fryer (about 3 pounds) cut in serving-size pieces
½ teaspoon salt
⅛ teaspoon pepper
1 clove garlic, minced
1 can (about 1 pound) tomatoes
1 tablespoon vinegar
½ teaspoon rosemary
½ teaspoon sugar

1. Sauté onion in 1 tablespoon salad oil in large frying pan about 5 minutes; remove and save for Step 3.

2. Sprinkle chicken with salt and pepper; brown in same frying pan with remaining 2 tablespoons oil and garlic.

3. Return onion to pan; add remaining ingredients; cover tightly. Simmer 40 minutes, or until chicken is tender.

CHICKEN CACCIATORE

Men especially like this zesty Italian dish. It's also a good choice for guests, because it waits well.

Makes 8 servings.

2 broiler-fryers (about 3 pounds each), quartered
3/4 cup flour
3 teaspoons salt
1/4 teaspoon pepper
6 tablespoons olive oil or salad oil
2 medium-size onions, chopped (1 cup)
1 clove garlic, minced
1 can (about 2 pounds) Italian tomatoes
1 tablespoon sugar
1 teaspoon basil
1/2 teaspoon thyme
2 medium-size green peppers, halved, seeded, and sliced

1. Wash chicken quarters; pat dry. Shake with flour, salt, and pepper in a paper bag to coat well.
2. Brown pieces, a few at a time, in olive oil or salad oil in a large frying pan; remove all from pan.
3. Stir onion and garlic into drippings in pan and sauté until soft; stir in tomatoes, sugar, basil, and thyme; heat to boiling.
4. Return chicken to pan; spoon some of the tomato sauce over; lay sliced green peppers on top; cover.
5. Simmer, basting several times with sauce in pan, 1½ hours, or until chicken is tender.

ROMAN FORUM CHICKEN

Flavorful bright red pimientos, black olives, mushrooms, a little white wine blend in this tempting Roman chicken-spaghetti dish.

Makes 6 servings.

2 broiler-fryers (2¹/₂ to 3 pounds each), cut in serving-size pieces
1 cup flour seasoned with 2 teaspoons salt and 1/4 teaspoon pepper
1/4 cup olive oil
1 clove garlic, mashed
1/4 cup chopped parsley
1/2 teaspoon poultry seasoning
1 teaspoon salt
1/8 teaspoon pepper
Dash red-pepper seasoning
1 cup dry white wine
3/4 cup black olives, sliced, pitted
1 can (6 ounces) sliced mushrooms, drained
1 can or jar (7 ounces) whole pimientos, drained and cut into large pieces
Parsley-Buttered Spaghetti

1. Roll chicken pieces in seasoned flour, then brown in hot oil in large heavy skillet..
2. Mix garlic, parsley, seasonings, and wine; pour over browned chicken; simmer a few minutes.
3. Scatter olives, mushrooms, and pimiento pieces over chicken. Cover skillet and cook over moderately low heat about 35 minutes, or until chicken pieces are fork-tender.
4. Serve hot with Parsley-Buttered Spaghetti.

PARSLEY-BUTTERED SPAGHETTI: Cook 1 package (8 ounces) thin spaghetti according to package directions. Drain and toss with about 1/4 pound melted butter or margarine (1 stick) and sprinkle with 1 cup chopped parsley.

FLORENTINE CHICKEN

Spinach takes on new elegance in this Italian chicken-cheese recipe.

Makes 4 servings.

1 package (10 ounces) frozen chopped spinach
3 tablespoons butter or margarine
3 tablespoons flour
1 teaspoon monosodium glutamate
1 teaspoon salt
Dash cayenne pepper
1½ cups milk
¼ cup grated Parmesan cheese
½ cup light cream
2 cups diced, cooked chicken
⅓ cup dry bread crumbs

1. Cook spinach, drain well, and transfer to 1½-quart baking dish.
2. Melt 2 tablespoons butter or margarine in saucepan. Stir in flour, monosodium glutamate, and cayenne. Gradually add milk and cook, stirring constantly, until mixture thickens and comes to a boil.
3. Add cheese and cream; cook over low heat until cheese is melted. Add chicken; pour cream mixture over spinach. Sprinkle with bread crumbs, dot with remaining butter.
4. Place under broiler and heat until lightly browned.

CHICKEN PAPRIKASH

The esteemed concoction of paprika-flavored chicken in sour cream with noodles is one of Hungary's great contributions to the world of food.

Makes 6 servings.

2 broiler-fryers (about 2 pounds each), cut up
⅓ cup plus 2 tablespoons flour
2 teaspoons salt
2 tablespoons paprika
3 tablespoons bacon fat
1 large onion, chopped (1 cup)
1¼ cups water
2 tablespoons butter or margarine
⅔ cup milk
1 cup (8-ounce carton) dairy sour cream
Cooked hot noodles

1. Shake chicken pieces with the ⅓ cup flour, 1½ teaspoons of the salt, and 1 tablespoon of the paprika in a paper bag to coat well. (Set remaining 1 tablespoon paprika and ½ teaspoon salt aside for making sauce.) Brown pieces slowly, a few pieces at a time, in bacon fat in a large frying pan; remove from pan.

2. Stir onion into pan; sauté until soft. Stir in ½ cup of the water; heat to boiling. Return chicken to pan; cover. Simmer 30 minutes, or until tender.
3. While chicken cooks, melt butter or margarine in a medium-size saucepan; stir in remaining 1 tablespoon paprika and ½ teaspoon salt, and the 2 tablespoons flour. Cook, stirring constantly, just until bubbly. Stir in milk and remaining ¾ cup water; continue cooking and stirring until sauce thickens and boils 1 minute.
4. Stir a generous ½ cup of the hot mixture into sour cream in a small bowl; stir back into remaining sauce in pan. Heat very slowly but do not let sauce boil (sour cream may curdle).
5. Spoon cooked noodles onto a heated serving platter; arrange chicken on top; spoon sauce over all.

CHICKEN KIEV

These spectacular Russian-style chicken breasts take fussing, so fix them ahead for a special dinner.

Makes 6 servings.

1½ sticks (6 ounces) butter or margarine
6 whole chicken breasts (about 12 ounces each)
4 tablespoons finely chopped parsley
½ teaspoon sugar
2 eggs
1 cup fine dry bread crumbs
1 teaspoon salt
⅛ teaspoon pepper
Shortening or salad oil for frying

1. Cut butter or margarine into 12 even-length sticks; chill in freezer while fixing chicken, for butter should be very cold.
2. Pull skin from chicken breasts; halve breasts and cut meat in one piece from bones. Place each half, boned side up, between waxed paper and pound very thin with a mallet or rolling pin to form a "cutlet." (Be careful not to pound holes in meat.)
3. Place 1 piece very cold butter or margarine, 1 teaspoon parsley, and a dash of the sugar on end of each cutlet; fold sides over to seal in butter, then roll up. Hold in place with wooden picks.
4. Beat eggs slightly in a pie plate; mix bread crumbs, salt, and pepper in a second pie plate. Dip stuffed rolls in egg, then in crumb mixture to coat well. Chill at least an hour. (This much can be done ahead.)
5. When ready to fry, melt enough shortening or pour in enough salad oil to make a 2-inch depth in an electric deep-fat fryer or large saucepan; heat to 350°.
6. Fry rolls, 3 or 4 at a time and turning often, 7 minutes, or until tender and crisply golden. Lift out with a slotted spoon; drain well. Keep hot until all rolls are cooked.

ARROZ CON POLLO

Chicken with rice, Spanish style, includes tomatoes, onion, mushrooms, pimientos — and a nip of garlic.

Bake at 350° for 1 hour and 10 minutes.
Makes 4 servings.

1 broiler-fryer (about 3 pounds), cut up
¼ cup salad or olive oil
1 cup raw rice
1 large onion, chopped (1 cup)
2 cloves garlic, minced
1 strand saffron, crushed
2 cans (about 1 pound each) tomatoes
1 can (3 or 4 ounces) chopped mushrooms
1 can (about 4 ounces) pimientos, diced
2 tablespoons chopped parsley
1½ teaspoons salt
⅛ teaspoon pepper

1. Brown chicken on all sides in hot oil in large heavy frying pan; drain on absorbent paper; place in 3-quart baking dish; save for Step 4.
2. Sauté rice in same frying pan, stirring often, about 5 minutes, or until golden-brown; add onion and garlic; sauté over low heat 10 minutes, or just until tender.
3. Stir in saffron, tomatoes, mushrooms, diced pimientos, parsley, salt, and pepper; heat to boiling, stirring often.
4. Pour hot tomato mixture over chicken in casserole; cover.
5. Bake in moderate oven (350°) 30 minutes; uncover; bake 40 minutes longer, or until rice and chicken are tender and liquid is absorbed.

Quick and Easy

CATALAN CHICKEN

1 roasting chicken (3½ to 4 pounds), cut up in serving-size pieces
3 tablespoons olive oil
1 teaspoon salt
3 medium-size onions, sliced (1½ cups)
4 canned pimientos, sliced
2 medium-size tomatoes, peeled and chopped
2 tablespoons tomato paste
¼ cup water
¼ cup dry sherry
½ teaspoon sugar

Simmer and serve this rich Spanish dish in your most colorful kettle.
Makes 4 servings.

1. In a large kettle, brown the chicken pieces in the olive oil with the salt. Remove chicken and set aside.
2. Put the sliced onions in the pan and cook until soft.
3. Add all the remaining ingredients and bring to a boil; return chicken to kettle and simmer, covered, 35 to 40 minutes, or until fork-tender.

AFRICAN CHICKEN

The once-dark continent isn't so remote these days, and the names of emerging nations are becoming as familiar to us as the well-traveled places of Europe and the Americas. We are learning more of African culture, including the cuisine. Here are two unusual chicken recipes from Africa — one from a brand new nation, one from an ancient Arab land. A French West African soup from Senegal can be found in the section on Soups.

UGANDA PEANUT BUTTER CHICKEN

Africans often use peanuts in cooking; we can get the same results with peanut butter. The taste is odd and exotic, but people who love peanut flavor will go for it.

Makes 6 servings.

2 broiler-fryers (about 2 pounds each), cut in serving-size pieces
¼ cup vegetable oil
2 teaspoons salt
1 teaspoon curry powder
1 large onion, peeled and sliced
1 large sweet red pepper, halved, seeded, and cut in strips
1 large tomato, sliced thin
1½ cups uncooked rice
¼ cup crunchy peanut butter
¼ cup warm water

1. Brown chicken pieces, part at a time, in vegetable oil in a Dutch oven or large frying pan; remove and set aside.
2. Stir salt and curry powder into drippings in Dutch oven; cook 1 minute. Stir in onion, red pepper, and tomato; cover. Simmer 5 minutes.
3. Return chicken to Dutch oven; cover again. Simmer 30 minutes, or until chicken is tender.
4. While chicken cooks, cook rice, following label directions; spoon onto a large deep serving platter. Arrange chicken on top; keep warm.
5. Blend peanut butter with warm water in a cup; stir into vegetable mixture in Dutch oven; heat to boiling. Spoon over chicken and rice.

TAGINE

In Morocco, ginger, paprika, and olives are favorite seasoners for the ever-popular chicken.

Makes 6 servings.

2 **broiler-fryers (about 2 pounds each), cut up**
4 **tablespoons (¹/₂ stick) butter or margarine**
4 **medium-size onions, chopped (2 cups)**
3 **teaspoons salt**
1¹/₂ **teaspoons ground ginger**
1 **teaspoon paprika**
¹/₄ **teaspoon pepper**
Water
1 **jar (7 ounces) stuffed green olives, drained and sliced**
2 **tablespoons flour**
Bulgar
¹/₄ **cup chopped parsley**
6 **thin lemon wedges**

1. Wash chicken pieces; pat dry. Brown, a few pieces at a time, in butter or margarine in a heavy kettle or Dutch oven; remove all from kettle.
2. Stir onions into drippings in kettle; sauté until soft. Stir in salt, ginger, paprika, pepper, and 1 cup water. Return chicken; cover.
3. Simmer, basting several times with liquid in kettle, 45 minutes, or until chicken is tender.
4. While chicken simmers, combine sliced olives with water to cover in a small saucepan; heat to boiling; drain. Keep hot for Step 7.

5. Remove chicken from kettle; keep hot. Pour liquid into a 2-cup measure; let stand about 1 minute, or until fat rises to top, then skim off. Add water to liquid, if needed, to make 1¹/₂ cups; return to kettle; heat to boiling.
6. Blend flour and ¹/₄ cup water until smooth in a cup; stir into boiling liquid. Cook, stirring constantly, until gravy thickens and boils in 1 minute.
7. When ready to serve, combine olives with Bulgar; spoon onto a heated serving platter; arrange chicken on top; sprinkle with chopped parsley. Arrange lemon wedges, petal fashion, in center. Pass gravy separately.

BULGAR
(Cracked Wheat)
Makes 6 servings.

3¹/₂ **cups water**
¹/₂ **cup (1 stick) butter or margarine**
3 **teaspoons salt**
1 **package (1 pound) bulgar wheat**
2 **medium-size eggplants**
1 **large onion, chopped (1 cup)**
¹/₄ **cup vegetable oil**

1. Heat water with butter or margarine and 2 teaspoons of the salt to boiling in a large heavy saucepan; slowly stir in bulgar wheat. Cook, stirring several times, 5 minutes, or until liquid is almost absorbed; cover.
2. Continue cooking very slowly, stirring several times with a fork, 45 minutes, or until wheat is very light and fluffy.
3. While wheat cooks, slice eggplants 1 inch thick; pare and cut into 1-inch cubes.
4. In a large frying pan sauté onion in vegetable oil until soft; stir in eggplant and remaining 1 teaspoon salt; cover. Cook slowly, stirring often, 30 minutes, or until eggplant is tender.
5. Add cooked wheat; toss lightly with two forks to mix well and to fluff up the wheat.

Chinese Chicken Salad

ORIENTAL CHICKEN

Most Americans love Oriental food — especially Chinese. Japanese cuisine also has its devotees, and for many people, true bliss comes only with a good curry. The spice importers have obliged by making once-rare seasonings available to us nationwide. Included with the Chinese and Japanese dishes here are a coconut-flavored chicken dish from Malaya and an Indian curry. You can also try, if you wish, Chicken Breasts Mandalay and South Pacific Chicken Breasts, in the CHICKEN BREASTS section, and Streamlined Chinese Chicken in CHICKEN ON A DIET.

MANDARIN SUPPER

Cubed chicken, Chinese-style fried rice, and soy-seasoned broccoli make this meal-in-a-skillet.

Makes 6 servings.

- 2 **chicken breasts (about 12 ounces each)**
- 1 **tablespoon packaged shrimp spice**
- 1 **tablespoon instant minced onion**
- 1 **teaspoon salt**
- 2 **cups water**
- 1 **cup uncooked rice**
- 1 **bunch fresh broccoli (about 1½ pounds)**
- 2 **large onions, chopped (2 cups)**
- 6 **tablespoons peanut oil or vegetable oil**
- 4 **tablespoons soy sauce**
- 2 **tablespoons wine vinegar or cider vinegar**
- ¼ **teaspoon ground ginger**
- ¼ **cup coarsely chopped salted peanuts**

1. Combine chicken breasts, shrimp spice, instant onion, salt, and water in a large saucepan; cover. Simmer 30 minutes, or until chicken is tender. Remove from broth and cool until easy to handle. Strain broth into a 4-cup measure; add water if needed to make 2¼ cups. Pull skin from chicken and take meat from bones; cut meat into large cubes.

2. Combine the 2¼ cups chicken broth and rice in a medium-size saucepan. Cook 25 minutes, or until rice is tender and liquid is absorbed.

3. While rice cooks, trim broccoli; split any large stalks lengthwise, then cut into 2-inch lengths. Cook in boiling salted water in a medium-size saucepan 15 minutes, or until crisply tender; drain; keep warm.

4. Sauté chopped onions in 4 tablespoons of the peanut oil or vegetable oil until soft in a large frying pan; stir in cooked rice. Sauté, stirring constantly, 5 minutes; add chicken; toss lightly to mix. Arrange cooked broccoli around edge in pan.

5. Combine remaining 2 tablespoons peanut oil or vegetable oil, soy sauce, wine vinegar or cider vinegar, and ginger in a cup; drizzle over broccoli. Sprinkle peanuts over rice. Serve warm right from the skillet it cooked in.

CHINESE CHICKEN SALAD

Chinese fried noodles and soy dressing give the touch of authenticity to this Oriental-style salad.

Makes 6 servings.

1 whole broiler-fryer (about 3 pounds)
2 cups water
Handful of celery tops
1 teaspoon salt
6 peppercorns
1¹/₂ cups Soy Dressing
1 bunch fresh broccoli (about 2 pounds)
6 cups broken salad greens
1 cup chopped celery
2 green onions, sliced
5 large radishes, sliced
1 can (3 ounces) Chinese fried noodles
1 hard-cooked egg, shelled

1. Simmer chicken with water, celery tops, salt, and peppercorns in kettle 1 hour, or until tender. Take chicken from broth and let drain in shallow pan just until cool enough to handle. (Strain broth and save for soup.)

2. Remove skin from chicken, then pull meat from frame in large pieces. (It comes off easily while still warm.) Cut into bite-size pieces; place in shallow pan; pour ¼ cup Soy Dressing over. Cover; chill at least an hour to blend flavors.

3. Trim and discard outer leaves from broccoli. Cut off ends to make about 4-inch-long stalks; split large ones lengthwise. Cook, covered, in about 1-inch depth boiling salted water in large frying pan 15 minutes, or until crisply tender; drain well.

4. Place in shallow pan; pour ½ cup Soy Dressing over. Cover; chill at least an hour.

5. When ready to serve, pile salad greens, celery, green onions, and radishes, saving about 8 slices for Step 7, into large shallow salad bowl. Pour remaining ¾ cup Soy Dressing over; toss lightly to mix.

6. Arrange marinated broccoli with stems toward center in a ring on top; fill ring with marinated chicken. Spoon noodles around broccoli.

7. Press white of egg, then yolk through a sieve onto separate sheets of waxed paper. Spoon white on top of chicken; top with saved radish slices, overlapping slightly; garnish with sieved egg yolk.

SOY DRESSING: Combine ½ cup soy sauce, ½ cup salad oil or peanut oil, and ½ cup wine vinegar or cider vinegar with 1 teaspoon salt and ½ teaspoon ground ginger in small jar with tight-fitting cover; shake to mix well. Makes 1½ cups.

CLASSIC CHICKEN ALMOND

An Oriental favorite of white meat, delicate vegetables, and toasted nuts. You can start it the day before, finish it up quickly at suppertime.

Makes 6 servings.

3 whole chicken breasts (about 12 ounces each), halved
1 large onion, peeled and sliced
1¹/₂ teaspoons salt
¹/₈ teaspoon pepper
Water
2 tablespoons vegetable oil
1¹/₂ cups chopped celery
1 package (10 ounces) frozen peas
1 can (3 or 4 ounces) sliced mushrooms
2 tablespoons cornstarch
¹/₂ teaspoon ground ginger
2 tablespoons soy sauce
Toasted slivered almonds (from a 5-ounce can)

1. Combine chicken breasts, 2 slices of the onion, salt, pepper, and 1 cup water in a large saucepan; cover. Simmer 20 minutes, or until chicken is tender.
2. Remove from broth and cool until easy to handle; strain broth into a small bowl. Pull skin from chicken and take meat from bones in one piece; chill, then cut into thin strips. Chill broth separately, then skim fat, if needed.

3. When ready to finish cooking, sauté remaining onion in vegetable oil in a large frying pan 2 to 3 minutes; push to side. Stir in celery and sauté 2 to 3 minutes; push to side. Place peas, mushrooms and liquid, and chicken strips in separate piles in pan; pour in broth; cover. Steam 10 minutes, or until peas are crisply tender.
4. Lift vegetables from pan with a slotted spoon; place in a serving bowl; lift out chicken strips and arrange on top of the vegetables.
5. Blend cornstarch and ginger with soy sauce in a cup; stir in 2 tablespoons water until smooth. Stir into liquid in pan; cook, stirring constantly, until sauce thickens and boils 3 minutes.
6. Spoon over chicken and vegetables; sprinkle with almonds. Garnish with thin strips of pimiento and drained canned mushroom caps and celery slices threaded onto kebab sticks, and serve with hot cooked rice or noodles, if you wish.

MAKE-AHEAD NOTE: Chicken may be cooked as much as a day ahead and chilled in its broth to keep moist. Chop celery ahead too, and place in a transparent bag in the refrigerator until ready to cook.

CHICKEN EGG ROLLS

What Chinese-food-lovers dream of. Fill the rolls and chill overnight — this makes them extra crisp.

Makes 6 servings, 2 rolls each.

FILLING

1 large onion, diced (1 cup)
1 cup thinly sliced celery
1 teaspoon salad oil
1 tablespoon soy sauce
2 cups diced cooked chicken OR 2 cans (5 to 6 ounces each) boned chicken, diced

PANCAKES

4 eggs
1½ cups water
1½ cups sifted flour
1 teaspoon salt
Peanut oil or salad oil
Sweet-and-Pungent Sauce

1. Make filling: Combine onion, celery, and salad oil in a small saucepan; cover. Cook over low heat 10 minutes, or until soft. Stir in soy sauce; pour over chicken in a medium-size bowl; toss to mix well. Let stand while making pancakes.
2. Make pancakes: Beat eggs with water until foamy in a medium-size bowl; beat in flour and salt just until smooth. (Batter will be thin.)
3. Heat an 8-inch frying pan slowly; test temperature by sprinkling in a few drops of water. When drops bounce about, temperature is right. Add about 1 teaspoon peanut oil or salad oil, tilting pan to cover bottom completely.
4. Pour batter, ¼ cup for each pancake, into pan. Bake 1 to 2 minutes, or until top appears dry and underside is golden. Lift out onto paper toweling to cool. (Only one side is baked.) Repeat with remaining batter, adding a little oil before each baking, to make 12 pancakes; cool each separately on paper toweling.
5. When ready to fill, spoon ¼ cup chicken mixture slightly off center on baked side of each pancake. Fold short end up over filling, then fold both sides toward center and roll up, jellyroll fashion, to cover filling completely; fasten with one or two wooden picks. Place in a shallow dish; cover. Chill overnight.
6. When ready to cook, heat a 1½-inch depth of peanut oil or salad oil to 400° in an electric skillet or deep heavy frying pan. Drop in chilled rolls, 2 or 3 at a time; fry, turning once, 5 to 8 minutes, or until golden. Drain on paper toweling. Keep rolls hot in warm oven until all are cooked. Remove picks; serve rolls plain or with Sweet-and-Pungent Sauce.

SWEET-AND-PUNGENT SAUCE

Makes 1¼ cups.

¼ cup firmly packed brown sugar
2 tablespoons cornstarch
¼ teaspoon ground ginger
1¼ cups water
¼ cup cider vinegar
2 tablespoons soy sauce

1. Mix brown sugar, cornstarch, and ginger in a small saucepan; stir in water until smooth. Cook, stirring constantly, until mixture thickens and boils 3 minutes. Remove from heat.
2. Stir in vinegar and soy sauce. Serve warm over egg rolls.

Quick and Easy   HONG KONG CHICKEN ALMOND

A simple version of the traditional Oriental dish.

Makes 4 servings.

2 **whole chicken breasts (about 12 ounces each)**
3 **tablespoons salad oil**
1 **cup sliced celery**
$1/2$ **clove garlic, minced**
2 **envelopes instant chicken broth
   OR 2 chicken bouillon cubes**
$1^1/2$ **cups water**
1 **tablespoon soy sauce**
1 **tablespoon chopped crystallized ginger**
1 **package (8 ounces) frozen Chinese
   pea pods**
2 **tablespoons cornstarch**
$1/4$ **cup toasted slivered almonds (from a
   5-ounce can)**
3 **cups hot cooked rice**

1. Pull skin from chicken breasts; halve breasts and cut meat in one piece from bones, then slice meat into long thin strips.
2. Heat salad oil in a large frying pan; add chicken and sauté, stirring constantly, 5 minutes. Stir in celery and garlic; sauté 3 minutes longer, or until chicken is almost tender.
3. Stir in chicken broth or bouillon cubes, water, soy sauce, and ginger; heat to boiling, crushing cubes, if using, with a spoon; add frozen pea pods; cover. Simmer 5 minutes.
4. Smooth cornstarch with a little water to a paste in a cup; stir into chicken mixture. Cook, stirring constantly, until mixture thickens and boils 3 minutes.
5. Spoon into a serving dish; sprinkle with almonds. Serve with rice.

CHICKEN TEMPURA

This delicately cooked Japanese-style chicken has a golden-rich batter coating.

Makes 8 servings.

2 **broiler-fryers (2 to 3 pounds each)**
2 **cups water**
2 **teaspoons salt**
1 **teaspoon poultry seasoning**
$1/4$ **teaspoon pepper**
2 **eggs**
$1/2$ **cup milk**
1 **cup sifted flour**
Fat for frying

1. Cut each chicken into 8 pieces (2 breasts, 2 wings, 2 thighs, 2 drumsticks); cook 15 minutes in 2 cups water seasoned with 1 teaspoon salt, poultry seasoning, and pepper. (Save broth to simmer backs, necks, and giblets to make soup for another meal.)
2. Drain chicken on paper towels; remove all skin and cut out any small rib bones; dry thoroughly.

3. Beat eggs slightly with milk in medium-size bowl; beat in flour and 1 teaspoon salt until smooth.
4. Melt enough fat (about 3 pounds) to make a 2-inch depth in large heavy saucepan; heat to 375°, or use an electric fryer, following manufacturer's directions.
5. Dip chicken, one piece at a time, into batter (tongs are a useful tool); let any excess batter drip back into bowl; fry 2 or 3 pieces at a time, turning once, about 4 minutes, or until golden; drain on paper towels; keep hot in warm oven while frying remaining chicken.

CHICKEN TERIYAKI

A Japanese baked dish, very easy to fix; shoyu (soy sauce) gives a lovely taste.

Bake at 325° for 1 hour.

Makes 4 servings.

1 broiler-fryer (about 3 pounds), cut in
   serving-size pieces
1/2 cup soy sauce
1/2 cup dry white wine
1 clove garlic, chopped
2 tablespoons sugar
1/2 tablespoon ground ginger

1. Marinate chicken 1 hour in a mixture of all other ingredients.
2. Remove chicken from marinade, place in shallow baking dish, and bake uncovered in slow oven (325°) 1 hour or until fork-tender, basting with marinade 2 or 3 times while cooking.
3. Serve on a hot platter or serving dish.

KERALA CHICKEN CURRY

Based on a traditional Indian dish, a chicken curry with yogurt.

Makes 6 servings.

2 broiler-fryers (about 2 pounds each),
   cut in serving-size pieces
1/3 cup vegetable oil
1 large onion, chopped (1 cup)
1 large apple, pared, quartered, cored,
   and chopped
2 cloves garlic, minced
3 tablespoons flour
2 tablespoons curry powder
1 teaspoon ground ginger
1/2 teaspoon salt
2 envelopes instant chicken broth
   OR 2 chicken bouillon cubes
2 cups water
1 cup (8-ounce carton) yogurt

1. Brown chicken, part at a time, in vegetable oil in a large frying pan; remove and set aside.
2. Stir onion, apple, and garlic into drippings in frying pan; sauté until soft. Sprinkle flour over top, then blend in with curry powder, ginger, and salt; cook 2 minutes. Stir in chicken broth or bouillon cubes and water; cook, stirring constantly, until sauce thickens and boils 1 minute.

3. Place chicken in sauce; cover. Simmer 35 minutes, or until chicken is tender; remove to a deep serving platter; keep warm.
4. Reheat sauce to boiling; simmer 5 minutes, or until slightly thickened; stir in yogurt. Heat *very slowly* just until hot; spoon over chicken. Serve with cooked rice, if you wish.

MALAY CHICKEN

Coconut milk is the something special in this exotic recipe.

Makes 8 servings.

4 whole chicken breasts (about 2¹/₂ pounds)
4 tablespoons (¹/₂ stick) butter or margarine
¹/₂ cup fresh coconut, grated, OR ¹/₂ cup canned, flaked coconut
3 medium-size onions (1¹/₂ cups), thinly sliced
1 tablespoon ground coriander
1 strand saffron
¹/₂ teaspoon chili powder
2 teaspoons salt
1¹/₂ teaspoons ground ginger
2 cloves garlic, minced
1 tablespoon grated lemon rind
1 tablespoon lime juice
1 teaspoon sugar
1 tablespoon cornstarch
2 cups Coconut Milk
1 package (1 pound) thin noodles

1. Bone chicken breasts and cut meat in cubes about 1¹/₂ inches.
2. Melt 2 tablespoons of the butter or margarine in a small skillet; lightly brown coconut. Remove.
3. Add remaining 2 tablespoons butter to skillet; add onions and sauté until lightly brown.
4. In a large saucepan, combine coconut, onions, coriander, saffron, chili powder, salt, ginger, garlic, lemon rind, lime juice, sugar, and chicken. Cook over low heat 5 minutes, stirring frequently.
5. Mix cornstarch and Coconut Milk; stir into saucepan. Cook over low heat 10 minutes or until chicken is tender. (Cover and keep warm over very low heat a few minutes, if necessary, until noodles are ready.)
6. While chicken-coconut mixture is cooking, boil noodles according to package directions. Drain and spoon into deep serving platter. Spoon chicken over.

COCONUT MILK

The sweet liquid that spills out when you crack a coconut is often called coconut milk, but that is not what is meant in recipes that call for coconut milk. The coconut milk used in cooking is an *infusion* of the coconut meat. You can make 2 cups coconut milk from fresh coconut or from canned, flaked coconut:

FRESH COCONUT MILK: Grate the meat of the coconut into a bowl. To each cup of coconut meat add 2 cups boiling water and let soak 30 minutes. Then squeeze through a piece of cheesecloth to extract all the liquid.

COCONUT MILK FROM CANNED, FLAKED COCONUT: To each cup of flaked coconut, add 2 cups hot milk. Let stand 30 minutes, then squeeze through cheesecloth to extract all the liquid.

Glazed Butterfly Chicken

CHICKEN POLYNESIAN

Chicken dishes from the Hawaiian Islands are influenced by the Orient, yet special in their way. As you would expect, the star ingredient is pineapple; prominent also are other citrus fruits, coconut, honey, curry, ginger, soy sauce, macadamia nuts. For a low-calorie Polynesian-style recipe, turn to Slim-Jim Hawaiian Chicken in the DIET section. And there is a fine Hawaiian Barbecue Sauce in SAUCES.

HAWAIIAN ROAST CHICKEN

A treat from the Aloha State, pineappley inside and out.

Roast at 375° for 1½ hours.

Makes 4 servings.

1 broiler-fryer (2¹/₂ to 3 pounds)
¹/₂ teaspoon poultry seasoning
¹/₄ teaspoon salt
3 tablespoons melted butter or margarine
¹/₂ cup water
2¹/₂ cups Hawaiian Stuffing
Golden Pineapple Glaze
Pineapple rings, grape clusters (optional)

1. Rinse chicken with cold water; drain and dry inside and outside. Rub inside cavity with the poultry seasoning and salt.
2. Stuff chicken with Hawaiian Stuffing, truss and brush with 3 tablespoons melted butter or margarine.
3. Place chicken on rack in roasting pan; add water and cover. Bake in a moderate (375°) oven about 1 hour.

4. Brush chicken with Golden Pineapple Glaze. Continue cooking, uncovered, brushing frequently with glaze, for ½ hour longer, or until drumstick-thigh joint moves easily.
5. To serve, garnish with pineapple rings and grape clusters, if you wish.

HAWAIIAN STUFFING: Combine 1½ cups soft bread crumbs, ⅓ cup flaked coconut, ¼ cup finely chopped celery, ¼ cup drained, crushed pineapple, 1 tablespoon grated orange peel, and 2 tablespoons melted butter or margarine in a bowl; toss lightly to blend. Makes about 2½ cups stuffing.

GOLDEN PINEAPPLE GLAZE: Combine ¼ cup pineapple syrup, ¼ cup orange juice, 2 tablespoons bottled meat sauce, 1 tablespoon melted butter or margarine. Makes about ¾ cup glaze.

POLYNESIAN HILO PLATTER

Many flavors join harmoniously in the stuffing and glaze of this exotic roast chicken.

Bake at 350° for 2 hours.

Makes 6 to 8 servings.

2 roasting chickens (about 4 pounds each)
4 cups Hilo Stuffing
3 tablespoons butter or margarine, melted
1¹/₂ cups Curry-Fruit Glaze

1. Rinse chickens inside and out with cold water; drain, then pat dry. Stuff neck and body cavities lightly with Hilo Stuffing. Smooth neck skin over stuffing and skewer to back; tie legs to tail with strings.
2. Place chickens on a rack in roasting pan; brush with melted butter or margarine.
3. Roast in moderate oven (350°) 1 hour.
4. Spoon part of the Curry-Fruit Glaze over each chicken to make a thick coating. Continue roasting, basting 2 or 3 times with remaining glaze, 1 hour, or until drumsticks move easily and chickens are glazed.
5. Remove to a heated serving platter; cut away strings and remove skewers. Garnish with flowers or leaves and serve hot.

HILO STUFFING

Makes 4 cups, or enough to stuff two 4-pound chickens.

1 cup uncooked white rice
4 tablespoons (¹/₂ stick) butter or margarine
1 medium-size onion, chopped (¹/₂ cup)
2 envelopes instant chicken broth OR 2 chicken bouillon cubes
2¹/₂ cups water
¹/₂ cup chopped macadamia nuts (from a 6-ounce jar)
¹/₂ cup flaked coconut

1. In a large saucepan, sauté rice in butter or margarine, stirring often, just until it is golden.

2. Stir in onion, chicken broth or bouillon cubes, and water; heat to boiling, crushing cubes, if using, with a spoon; cover. Simmer 20 minutes, or until rice is tender and liquid is absorbed.
3. Sprinkle with nuts and coconut; toss lightly to mix.

CURRY-FRUIT GLAZE

Makes 1¹/₂ cups, or enough to glaze two 4-pound chickens.

4 slices bacon, diced
1 medium-size onion, chopped (¹/₂ cup)
2 tablespoons flour
1 tablespoon sugar
2 teaspoons curry powder
¹/₂ teaspoon salt
1 tablespoon bottled steak sauce
1 cup water
2 tablespoons lemon juice
1 jar (4 ounces) baby-pack strained apples-and-apricots

1. Sauté bacon until almost crisp in a medium-size saucepan; remove and drain on paper toweling.
2. Stir onions into drippings in saucepan; sauté until just soft. Stir in flour, sugar, curry powder, and salt; heat until bubbly.
3. Stir in remaining ingredients and bacon. Simmer, stirring several times, 15 minutes, or until thick.

CHICKEN MAUI

A delicious Hawaiian concoction, high in flavor and texture.

Makes 4 servings.

1 broiler-fryer (about 3 pounds), quartered
3 cups water
2 teaspoons salt
¼ teaspoon pepper
1 medium-size onion, chopped
3 tablespoons salad oil
1¼ cups shredded green cabbage
½ cup diced celery
¾ cup coarsely chopped macadamia nuts
OR ¾ cup toasted, slivered almonds
2 tablespoons soy sauce
1 cup drained pineapple chunks
1 tablespoon honey

1. Put chicken in a kettle with water, salt, pepper, and chopped onion. Simmer gently 35 minutes until chicken is tender.
2. Remove chicken; strain and reserve broth. Cool chicken until easy to handle. Bone chicken and cut meat into small pieces.

3. Heat oil in a deep skillet; sauté cabbage, celery, and chicken about 3 minutes. Gradually add nuts, soy sauce, and 2 cups reserved broth, stirring constantly. Simmer, covered, over medium heat 5 minutes.
4. Add pineapple and honey; cook 3 minutes longer. Serve on a hot platter.

GLAZED BUTTERFLY CHICKEN

For the all-out Hawaii buff: Chicken breasts, fragrant with a fruit-curry glaze and frilly with coconut.

Bake at 350° for 1½ hours.

Makes 8 servings.

Curry-Fruit Glaze (from Polynesian Hilo Platter, opposite page)
8 whole chicken breasts (about 12 ounces each)
6 tablespoons (¾ stick) butter or margarine
1 teaspoon ground ginger
½ cup flaked coconut

1. Make Curry-Fruit Glaze and set aside until needed for Step 3.

2. Cut away rib bones from chicken with sharp knife or scissors, leaving the V-shape bone at neck.
3. Melt butter or margarine in a large shallow baking pan; stir in ginger. Roll chicken in mixture to coat well, then arrange, skin side up, in a single layer in pan. Tuck edges of each breast under to given a rounded shape. Spoon glaze over to make a very thick coating.
4. Bake uncovered in moderate oven (350°), basting often with glaze mixture in pan, 1 hour and 20 minutes, or until richly glazed and tender.
5. Top each breast with a sprinkling of coconut; bake 10 minutes longer, or until lightly toasted.

105

Peachy Low-Calorie Chicken

CHICKEN ON A DIET

Chicken is a wise choice for weight-worriers because, pound for pound, it has the lowest calorie count — and lowest fat content — of almost any popular meat. Chicken dishes offer welcome variety, for the meat can be paired up with many other foods while the total calorie count is kept within bounds. Here are nine interesting chicken recipes, each with the calories per portion, to help you eat well while keeping slim.

SLIM-JIM HAWAIIAN CHICKEN

Cooked to a turn in a zippy soy-and-onion sauce. No fat needed.

Bake at 350° for 1½ hours.

Makes 6 servings.

3 small broiler-fryers (about 1½ pounds each)
1 small onion, chopped (¼ cup)
¼ cup soy sauce
1½ cups water
6 slices diet-pack pineapple (from a 1-pound, 4-ounce can)
2 tablespoons chopped parsley

1. Arrange split chickens, skin side down, in a large shallow baking pan. Mix onion, soy sauce, and water in a small bowl; pour over chicken.
2. Bake in moderate oven (350°) 45 minutes; turn chicken; bake, basting several times with soy mixture in pan, 45 minutes longer, or until brown and tender.
3. Drain pineapple slices well on paper toweling; roll edge of each in chopped parsley. Serve with chicken.

Dieter's portion: 1 chicken half with 1 pineapple slice — 287 calories.

PEACHY LOW-CALORIE CHICKEN

Chicken pieces baked with fruit and a seasoned glaze that add almost no calories.

Bake at 400° about 1 hour.

Makes 6 servings.

3 whole chicken breasts, split
3 chicken drumsticks
3 chicken thighs
1 can (about 1 pound) diet-pack cling peach halves
2 tablespoons lemon juice
1 teaspoon soy sauce

1. Arrange chicken pieces in a single layer in shallow baking dish, 12x8x2.
2. Drain peach syrup into a cup (save halves for Step 3). Add lemon juice and soy sauce to syrup; brush about half over chicken.
3. Bake in hot oven (400°), brushing every 15 minutes with remaining peach syrup mixture and pan juices, 1 hour, or until chicken is tender and richly browned. Place peach halves around chicken; brush with pan juices; bake 5 minutes longer to heat peaches.

Dieter's portion: ½ chicken breast, 1 drumstick or thigh, and ½ peach — 210 calories.

SKINNY-GIRL PAELLA

A low-calorie version of the favorite from sunny Valencia.

Bake at 350° for 1 hour.

Makes 6 servings.

1 broiler-fryer (about 2 pounds), cut in serving-size pieces
1 large onion, chopped (1 cup)
1 clove garlic, minced
1 cup uncooked rice
6 small slices salami (about 2 ounces), diced
2 teaspoons salt
1 teaspoon sugar
1/4 teaspoon pepper
1/8 teaspoon crushed saffron
1 can (about 1 pound) tomatoes
1 1/2 cups water
1 envelope instant chicken broth OR 1 chicken bouillon cube
1 pound fresh shrimps, shelled and deveined, OR 1 package (12 ounces) frozen deveined shelled raw shrimps
1 can (4 ounces) pimientos, drained and cut in large pieces

1. Pull skin from chicken pieces, if you wish. Place chicken, meaty side down, in a single layer on rack of broiler pan.
2. Broil, 4 inches from heat, 10 minutes; turn; broil 10 minutes longer, or until lightly browned; set aside for Step 4.
3. Pour drippings from broiler pan into a medium-size frying pan. Stir in onion and garlic; sauté until soft; spoon into a 12-cup baking dish with rice, salami, salt, sugar, pepper, and saffron.
4. Combine tomatoes with water and instant chicken broth or bouillon cube in same frying pan; heat to boiling, crushing bouillon cube, if used, with a spoon. Stir into rice mixture with shrimps. Arrange chicken and pimientos on top; cover.
5. Bake in moderate oven (350°) 1 hour, or until liquid is absorbed and chicken is tender. Garnish with parsley and serve with chopped green onions to sprinkle on top, if you wish.

Dieter's portion: 1/2 chicken breast, 5 shrimps, and 1 cup rice mixture — 406 calories.

NO-FAT FRY WITH ONIONS

5-25-68
very good

This magic chicken cooks golden brown with no fat, no turning.

Makes 4 servings.

1 broiler-fryer (about 2 pounds), cut in serving-size pieces
1 teaspoon salt
1/8 teaspoon pepper
2 large onions, sliced
1/2 cup water

1. Place chicken, skin side down, in a single layer in a large frying pan.
2. Sprinkle with salt and pepper; place onion slices on top; cover tightly. (No need to add any fat.)
3. Cook over low heat 30 minutes. Tilt lid slightly so liquid will evaporate; continue cooking 20 minutes longer, or until chicken is tender and golden.
4. Place chicken on a heated serving platter, pushing onions back into pan; stir in water, mixing with browned bits from bottom of pan; cook until liquid evaporates. Spoon over chicken.

Dieter's portion: 1/4 of the chicken and about 1/4 cup onions — 221 calories.

CHICKEN LITTLE

1 broiler-fryer (about 3 pounds), cut in
  serving-size pieces
1 teaspoon salt
1/8 teaspoon pepper
1/2 teaspoon paprika
2 tablespoons salad oil
Juice of 1/2 lemon
1/2 cup water
1/4 teaspoon each savory and thyme
1 clove garlic, minced
1 medium onion, sliced
1 medium green pepper, seeded and cut
  in strips
1/2 pound mushrooms

Savory skillet chicken for thin-thinking gourmets.
Makes 4 servings.

1. Sprinkle chicken with salt, pepper, and paprika. Heat oil in skillet. Place chicken, skin side down, in hot oil. Brown 20 minutes on both sides.
2. Add lemon juice, water, herbs, and garlic. Cover; cook 10 minutes. Add vegetables; cover and cook 10 minutes longer, or until chicken is tender.

Dieter's portion: 1/4 of the chicken and vegetables — 388 calories.

SLICK CHICK

Each dieter rates a half golden-glazed chicken plus spicy apple stuffing in this too-good-to-be-true roast.

Roast at 375° for 1 1/2 hours.
Makes 4 servings.

2 small whole broiler-fryers (about 1 1/2
  pounds each)
1 1/2 teaspoons salt
1 large onion, chopped (1 cup)
1/4 cup water
1/4 teaspoon ground coriander
1/4 teaspoon curry powder
3 medium-size apples, pared, quartered,
  cored, and chopped
Granulated or liquid no-calorie sweetener
1 teaspoon paprika
1/2 cup chicken broth

1. Rinse chickens inside and out with cold water; drain, then pat dry. Sprinkle insides with 1/2 teaspoon of the salt.
2. Simmer onion in water in a medium-size frying pan 5 minutes, or until soft; stir in coriander, curry powder, apples, another 1/2 teaspoon of the salt, and your favorite no-calorie sweetener, using the equivalent of 1 teaspoon sugar.

3. Cook, stirring often, over medium heat 10 minutes, or until apples are slightly soft. Remove from heat.
4. Stuff neck and body cavities of chickens lightly with apple mixture. Smooth neck skin over stuffing and skewer to back; tie legs to tail with string. Place chickens, side by side, in a roasting pan.
5. Mix remaining 1/2 teaspoon salt and paprika in cup; sprinkle over chickens.
6. Roast in moderate oven (375°), basting several times with chicken broth, 1 1/2 hours or until drumsticks move easily and meaty part of a thigh feels soft. (If you want to garnish chickens with onions, as shown in our picture, thread wedges of peeled onion onto dampened wooden picks and insert into chickens for last half hour of cooking time.)
7. Remove chickens to a heated serving platter; cut away strings and remove skewers. Garnish platter with parsley and a few thin apple slices, if you wish. Cut chickens in half, divide stuffing evenly.

Dieter's portion: 1/2 chicken plus half of stuffing from 1 chicken — 421 calories. (Crash dieters can omit the stuffing.)

WEIGHT-WORRIERS' FRICASSEE

A happy combination of rich-tasting gravy and sensible calorie count.

Makes 6 servings.

3 whole chicken breasts (about 12 ounces each), halved
1 small onion, chopped (¹/₄ cup)
¹/₂ cup finely chopped celery
2 teaspoons salt
¹/₈ teaspoon pepper
1 cup water
2 tablespoons instant-type flour
¹/₂ cup skim milk
Biscuit Crisps

1. Simmer chicken, covered, with onion, celery, salt, pepper, and water in a medium-size frying pan 30 minutes, or until tender; remove to a heated serving platter; keep hot while making gravy.
2. Mix flour and skim milk in a cup; stir into hot broth in pan. Cook, stirring constantly, until gravy thickens and boils 1 minute. Serve in a separate bowl.

BISCUIT CRISPS: Combine 1 cup sifted regular flour, 1½ teaspoons baking powder, and ¼ teaspoon salt in a medium-size bowl; cut in 2 tablespoons margarine with a pastry blender until mixture is crumbly. Add ⅓ cup skim milk all at once; stir lightly with a fork just until mixture is evenly moistened. Turn out onto a lightly floured pastry cloth or board; knead gently, flouring hands lightly, 5 or 6 times, then pat into a rectangle about ½ inch thick; cut into 6 squares. Place on a lightly greased cooky sheet; brush tops with skim milk. Bake in hot oven (425°) 10 to 12 minutes, or until lightly browned. Break apart with two forks for serving.

Dieter's portion: ½ chicken breast, 1 biscuit, and ¼ cup gravy — 272 calories.

STREAMLINED CHINESE CHICKEN

Meal-in-one teams white meat with pineapple and vegetables.

Makes 6 servings.

3 whole chicken breasts (about 2¹/₂ pounds)
3 tablespoons soy sauce
1 tablespoon salad oil or peanut oil
1 can (1 pint, 2 ounces) unsweetened pineapple juice
4 tablespoons cornstarch
1 can (8 ounces) diet-pack pineapple chunks
2 cans (3 or 4 ounces each) sliced mushrooms
¹/₂ teaspoon salt
1 package (10 ounces) frozen peas, thawed
6 cups shredded Chinese cabbage (about 1 head)
3 cups cooked hot rice

1. Remove skin and bones from chicken breasts; slice meat into long thin strips.
2. Place soy sauce in pie plate; dip chicken strips into sauce; brown quickly in salad oil or peanut oil in large frying pan.
3. Stir just enough unsweetened pineapple juice into cornstarch in cup to make a smooth paste; save for Step 5.
4. Stir remaining pineapple juice, and pineapple chunks and mushrooms with liquid into chicken in pan; heat to boiling.
5. Stir in cornstarch mixture and salt; cook, stirring constantly, until sauce thickens and boils 3 minutes. Cover; simmer 15 minutes.
6. Stir in peas; arrange cabbage on top. Cover; cook 8 minutes, or until peas and cabbage are tender. Serve over cooked hot rice.

Dieter's portion: 1 cup chicken mixture and ½ cup rice — 398 calories.

DIETER'S DELIGHT

A masterpiece, and fun to make: chilled chicken breasts in a gelatin glaze decorated with vegetable flowers.

Makes 6 servings.

3 chicken breasts (about 12 ounces each), halved
2 envelopes instant chicken broth OR
  2 chicken bouillon cubes
1¹/₂ cups water
3 teaspoons leaf tarragon
1 tablespoon instant minced onion
Few sprigs of parsley
1 envelope unflavored gelatin
6 carrot slices
2 green onion tops, cut in strips
Fresh spinach leaves

1. Combine chicken breasts, instant broth or bouillon cubes, and water in a large saucepan. Tie tarragon, onion, and parsley in a cheesecloth bag; add to saucepan; cover. Simmer 30 minutes, or until chicken is tender. Remove from broth and cool until easy to handle; pull off skin; chill. Chill broth until fat rises to top, then skim off.
2. Soften gelatin in ½ cup of the broth in a small saucepan; heat, stirring constantly, until gelatin dissolves; remove from heat. Stir in remaining broth.
3. Place chicken breasts in a single layer on a wire rack set in a shallow pan.
4. Measure ½ cup of the gelatin mixture; set cup in a small bowl of ice and water; chill just until as thick as unbeaten egg white. Brush over chicken breasts to coat evenly. (Keep remaining gelatin mixture at room temperature.)
5. Arrange a flower in gelatin on each chicken breast, using a carrot slice for blossom and a long strip of green onion top for stem and short pieces for leaves. Chill until firm.
6. Measure out another ½ cup of the gelatin mixture and chill until thickened; brush over decorations on chicken; chill until firm. Chill remaining gelatin mixture; brush over chicken a third time to make a thick coating, then chill several hours, or until firm.
7. When ready to serve, arrange chicken on a spinach-lined large platter. Garnish with cherry tomatoes, cut to form flowers, and top with snips of spinach, if you wish.

Dieter's portion: One-half chicken breast — 196 calories.

South Pacific Chicken Breasts

CHICKEN BREASTS

Breasts are the elegant part of a chicken, meaty and delicate, and the favorite of white-meat fanciers. You can buy chicken breasts separately in the supermarket and cook them — whole, halved, or boned — in a host of excellent recipes. Besides the choices here, see the many chicken breast recipes in the sections COMPANY'S COMING, ORIENTAL CHICKEN, and SALADS.

GOURMET CHICKEN BREASTS

Rich creamed chicken breasts are sparked with water chestnuts and pimientos for a fancy touch.

Makes enough for 2 meals, 4 servings each.

4 chicken breasts (about 12 ounces each)
1 small onion, quartered
Few celery tops
2 teaspoons salt
6 peppercorns
1¹/₂ cups water
¹/₂ cup (1 stick) butter or margarine
¹/₂ cup flour
¹/₄ teaspoon nutmeg
Dash of pepper
1 tablespoon lemon juice
2 pimientos, chopped
1 can (5 ounces) water chestnuts, drained
   and sliced
1 cup cream

1. Simmer chicken with onion, celery tops, 1 teaspoon of the salt, peppercorns, and water in a large saucepan 30 minutes, or until tender. Remove chicken from broth; cool until easy to handle. Strain broth into a 2-cup measure; add water, if needed, to make 2 cups; set aside for making the sauce in Step 3.
2. Remove skin from chickens, then pull chicken from bones; dice meat. (There should be about 4 cups.)
3. Melt butter or margarine in a large saucepan; blend in flour, remaining 1 teaspoon salt, nutmeg, and pepper; cook, stirring constantly, just until bubbly. Stir in the 2 cups chicken broth; continue cooking and stirring until sauce thickens and boils 1 minute. (It will be very thick.) Remove from heat.
4. Stir in lemon juice, diced chicken, pimiento, and water chestnuts.
5. Spoon half of mixture into a 6-cup freezer container; cool, cover, label, date, and freeze.
6. Stir cream very slowly into remaining mixture in saucepan. Heat, stirring often, just until hot. (If you prefer mixture thinner, stir in about ¹/₂ cup milk.) Spoon into patty shells, or over your choice of buttered toast, rice, or mashed potato.

Note: To heat frozen chicken, set container in a pan of hot water, replacing water as it cools, just until mixture is thawed enough to slide into top of a large double broiler. Add 2 tablespoons butter or margarine and 1 cup cream; heat, stirring several times, over simmering water, until hot. (Thin slightly with milk as above, if you wish.)

POULET GILBERT

Sour cream and zesty vegetables give plenty of flavor to delicate breast meat.

Makes 4 to 6 servings.

3 **chicken breasts (about 12 ounces each)**
1¹/₂ **cups water**
1 **teaspoon salt**
2 **cups chopped celery**
1 **large onion, chopped (1 cup)**
1 **medium-size green pepper, halved, seeded, and chopped**
4 **tablespoons (¹/₂ stick) butter or margarine**
2 **tablespoons flour**
2 **teaspoons paprika**
¹/₈ **teaspoon pepper**
1 **cup (8-ounce carton) dairy sour cream**

1. Combine chicken breasts, water, and ½ teaspoon of the salt in a large frying pan; heat to boiling; cover. Simmer 30 minutes, or until chicken is tender.
2. Remove from broth and cool until easy to handle. Pour broth into a 1-cup measure; add water, if needed, to make 1 cup. Pull skin from chicken and take meat from bones; dice meat.
3. Sauté celery, onion, and green pepper in butter or margarine until soft in same large frying pan; sprinkle flour, paprika, remaining ½ teaspoon salt, and pepper over top, then stir in; stir in the 1 cup chicken broth. Cook, stirring constantly, until sauce thickens and boils 1 minute.
4. Stir in diced chicken and sour cream. Heat *very slowly* just until hot. Serve over cooked noodles, if you wish.

CHICKEN BREASTS MORNAY

A nippy cheese sauce sparks bland and delicate white meat.

Bake at 350° for 55 to 60 minutes.

Makes 4 servings.

4 **chicken breasts**
¹/₄ **cup flour seasoned with**
  ¹/₂ **teaspoon salt and dash of pepper**
¹/₄ **cup (¹/₂ stick) melted butter or margarine**
Mornay Sauce

1. Dust chicken breasts with seasoned flour.
2. Place in small, shallow baking dish, skin side down; pour melted butter or margarine over and around chicken.
3. Bake in moderate oven (350°) 30 minutes; turn chicken breasts; bake 25 to 30 minutes longer, basting 2 or 3 times during baking, until chicken is golden-brown and tender when pierced with a fork.
4. Place on heated serving platter; serve with Mornay Sauce.

MORNAY SAUCE
Makes about 1¹/₄ cups.
2 **teaspoons butter or margarine**
2 **tablespoons flour**
¹/₂ **teaspoon salt**
¹/₈ **teaspoon pepper**
¹/₂ **cup milk**
¹/₂ **cup chicken stock**
³/₄ **cup grated sharp Cheddar cheese**
¹/₂ **teaspoon prepared mustard**
¹/₂ **teaspoon Worcestershire sauce**
1 **tablespoon chopped parsley**

1. Melt butter or margarine in small saucepan; remove from heat.
2. Blend in flour, salt, and pepper; stir in milk and chicken stock.
3. Cook over low heat, stirring constantly, until sauce thickens and boils 1 minute.
4. Add cheese, mustard, and Worcestershire sauce; continue cooking, stirring occasionally, until cheese melts; remove from heat.
5. Stir in parsley; serve hot.

CHICKEN BREASTS SUPREME

An easygoing concoction of creamed white meat baked over rice with a crust of buttery crumbs topping it all.

Bake at 400° for 20 minutes.

Makes 6 servings.

3 whole chicken breasts (about 2¹/₂ pounds)
3 cups water
1 teaspoon salt
4 peppercorns
Handful of celery tops
2 cups precooked rice
1 can (about 11 ounces) chicken gravy
1 tablespoon butter or margarine
¹/₂ cup ready-mix bread stuffing (from an 8-ounce package)

1. Combine chicken breasts with water, salt, peppercorns, and celery tops, in a medium-size saucepan; cover. Cook 20 minutes, or until tender. Strain broth into a 4-cup measure; pour in water, if necessary, to make 2½ cups.

2. Let chicken stand until cool enough to handle, then remove skin and bones; cut meat into serving-size pieces.

3. Cook rice in 2 cups of the broth in same saucepan, following label directions. Stir remaining ½ cup broth into chicken gravy in small saucepan; heat slowly just until bubbly.

4. Spoon rice into 8-cup baking dish; top with chicken pieces; pour gravy over. Melt butter or margarine in small saucepan; stir in bread stuffing. Sprinkle on top.

5. Bake in hot oven (400°) 20 minutes, or until bubbly-hot.

CHICKEN BREASTS MANDALAY

This delectable chicken has a light curry-and-fruit-flavored sauce.

Bake at 350° for 2 hours.

Makes 8 servings.

4 chicken breasts (about 12 ounces each)
3 tablespoons flour
1 tablespoon curry powder
2 teaspoons salt
4 tablespoons vegetable oil
1 tablespoon sugar
2 envelopes instant beef broth or 2 beef bouillon cubes
1 large onion, chopped (1 cup)
1 cup water
1 jar (about 5 ounces) baby-pack apricots
2 tablespoons lemon juice
2 teaspoons soy sauce

1. Pull skin from chicken breasts; halve each.

2. Shake with mixture of flour, curry powder, and salt in a paper bag to coat lightly and evenly.

3. Brown pieces in vegetable oil in a large frying pan; place in a 10-cup baking dish.

4. Stir sugar, beef broth or bouillon cubes, onion, water, apricots, lemon juice, and soy sauce into drippings in frying pan; heat to boiling, crushing bouillon cubes, if used, with a spoon. Pour over chicken.

5. Bake, covered, in moderate oven (350°) 1 hour, or until chicken is tender and sauce is bubbly hot. Serve over hot fluffy rice or noodles, if you wish.

Quick and Easy SHERRIED CHICKEN BREASTS

Lightly seasoned and swimming in sherry and milk, they will simmer themselves to a delicious turn with no help from you.

Makes 4 servings.

4 **chicken breasts (about 12 ounces each)**
2 **teaspoons salt**
¼ **teaspoon pepper**
1 **teaspoon paprika**
4 **tablespoons vegetable oil**
¾ **cup dry sherry**
1 **cup milk**
4 **tablespoons flour**

1. Sprinkle chicken breasts with 1 teaspoon of salt, pepper, and paprika.
2. Brown in vegetable oil in a large frying pan. Stir in sherry; heat to boiling; cover. Simmer 30 minutes, or until tender. Remove chicken to a heated deep serving platter; keep warm while making sauce.
3. Heat liquid in frying pan to boiling.
4. Blend milk into flour and remaining 1 teaspoon salt until smooth in a cup; stir into boiling liquid. Cook, stirring constantly, until sauce thickens and boils 1 minute. Pour over chicken breasts.

TENNESSEE CLUB CHICKEN

Southern-fried chicken breasts and ham, in a milky sauce lightly touched with sherry.

Bake at 350° for 45 minutes.
Makes 8 servings.

4 **chicken breasts (about 12 ounces each)**
8 **small thin slices cooked ham**
½ **cup flour**
1½ **teaspoons salt**
¼ **teaspoon pepper**
4 **tablespoons (½ stick) butter or margarine**
2½ **cups milk**
½ **cup dry sherry**

1. Halve chicken breasts; wash and pat dry. Cut a pocket, about 3 x 2, in thin side of each. Place breasts on waxed paper.
2. Sauté ham slices quickly in a large frying pan; cool slightly. Tuck one into pocket in each half chicken breast.
3. Mix ¼ cup of the flour, 1 teaspoon of the salt, and pepper in a cup; sprinkle over chicken to coat evenly.
4. Melt butter or margarine in frying pan used for ham; add chicken breasts and brown slowly; place in a large shallow baking dish.

5. Blend remaining ¼ cup flour and ½ teaspoon salt into drippings in pan; cook, stirring constantly, just until bubbly. Stir in milk; continue cooking and stirring, scraping brown bits from bottom of pan, until sauce thickens and boils 1 minute; stir in sherry. Pour over chicken breasts; cover.
6. Bake in moderate oven (350°) 45 minutes, or until chicken is tender.
7. Arrange chicken on a heated deep serving platter; spoon sauce over top. Garnish with parsley, if you wish.

SOUTH PACIFIC CHICKEN BREASTS

Fruity, spicy — a glorious example of Island cuisine.

Makes 6 servings.

6 **whole chicken breasts (about 12 ounces each)**
1 **tablespoon cinnamon**
1¹/₂ **teaspoons curry powder**
1¹/₂ **teaspoons garlic salt**
¹/₂ **cup honey**
³/₄ **cup grapefruit juice**
1 **can (about 8 ounces) crushed pineapple**

1. Place chicken breasts in a large frying pan or kettle. Blend cinnamon, curry powder, garlic salt, and honey in a 2-cup measure; stir in grapefruit juice; pour over chicken; cover.

2. Simmer, stirring liquid in bottom of pan often so honey won't scorch, 20 minutes, or until chicken is tender.
3. Remove from liquid, letting any excess drip back into pan; slip off skin, if you wish. Place chicken on broiler rack.
4. Stir pineapple and syrup into liquid in pan; brush over chicken.
5. Broil, 4 to 6 inches from heat, 5 minutes, or until lightly glazed.

CHICKEN AND MUSHROOM DUET

Tender chicken breasts with mushrooms and noodles in a creamy gravy.

Makes 6 servings.

3 **whole chicken breasts (2¹/₂ to 3 pounds), split**
2 **cups water**
1 **slice onion**
Handful of celery tops
1 **teaspoon salt**
4 **peppercorns**
1 **package (8 ounces) noodles**
¹/₂ **pound fresh mushrooms, sliced**
2 **tablespoons butter or margarine**
1 **can (about 11 ounces) chicken gravy**

1. Combine chicken breasts, water, onion, celery tops, salt, and peppercorns in large saucepan. Simmer, covered, 20 minutes, or until chicken is tender.
2. While chicken simmers, cook noodles in large amount boiling salted water, following label directions; drain; place in greased shallow 8-cup casserole.
3. Sauté mushrooms in butter or margarine in large frying pan; arrange in clusters on top of noodles. (Keep casserole warm in heated oven while browning the chicken and heating the gravy.)
4. Drain chicken breasts (strain broth and save for soup). Brown chicken quickly in same frying pan, adding more butter or margarine, if needed; place on noodles.
5. Stir chicken gravy into frying pan; heat to boiling; pour over and around chicken.

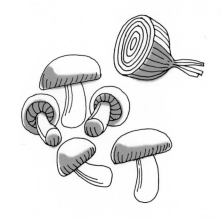

Drumstick Fricassee

DRUMSTICKS

Homemakers like drumstick recipes because chicken legs are juicy and meaty, ideal especially for families who prefer dark meat. Here is a lively quartet of drumstick dishes; see also Herb-Fried Drumsticks in CHICKEN FOR A CROWD.

STUFFED DRUMSTICKS NAPOLI

Each golden leg contains a zippy salami stuffing. Makes 8 servings.

8 chicken drumsticks with thighs (about 5 pounds)
1 piece (4 ounces) salami
1/2 cup flour
2 teaspoons salt
1 teaspoon paprika
1 teaspoon leaf oregano, crumbled
1/8 teaspoon pepper
1/2 cup vegetable oil

1. Cut through chicken legs at joints to separate drumsticks and thighs, then cut an opening along bone of each drumstick and in meaty part of each thigh to make a pocket for a salami slice.
2. Cut salami into 16 strips; stuff 1 strip into each piece of chicken.
3. Shake pieces, a few at a time, in mixture of flour, salt, paprika, oregano, and pepper in a paper bag to coat evenly.
4. Cook pieces slowly in vegetable oil in a large frying pan 20 minutes; turn; cover loosely. Cook 20 minutes longer, or until tender and crisply golden. Serve warm or cold.

DRUMSTICK FRICASSEE

Meaty chicken legs, sweet potato, and peas in rich gravy are topped with lemon-flecked dumplings. Makes 2 servings.

4 drumsticks (about 1 pound)
1/2 small onion, sliced
1/4 cup chopped celery tops
1 teaspoon salt
1/8 teaspoon pepper
1 1/2 cups water
2 teaspoons flour
1 large sweet potato, pared and sliced 1/2 inch thick
1 cup frozen peas (from a 1 1/2 pound bag)
Lemon Dumplings

1. Cook chicken with onions, celery tops, salt, and pepper in 1 cup water 30 minutes, or until tender.
2. Blend flour into 1/2 cup water; stir into broth; cook, stirring constantly, until gravy thickens and boils 1 minute.
3. Add potato and peas; heat to boiling, then simmer 10 minutes while making Lemon Dumplings.
4. Drop batter in 4 mounds on top of hot chicken and vegetables; cover tightly. Cook 20 minutes, or until dumplings are fluffy-light.
5. Lift off dumplings; spoon chicken, vegetables, and gravy into serving dishes; top with dumplings. Garnish with grated lemon rind, if you wish.

LEMON DUMPLINGS: Combine 2/3 cup sifted flour, 1 teaspoon baking powder, 1/2 teaspoon grated lemon rind, and 1/4 teaspoon salt. Stir 1 teaspoon lemon juice into 1/3 cup milk. (No need to fuss if mixture curdles.) Add all at once to dry ingredients; stir just until flour mixture is moistened completely.

DRUMSTICKS PIERRE

8 drumsticks (about 2 pounds)
$^1/_4$ cup flour seasoned with $^1/_2$ teaspoon
   salt and a dash of pepper
3 tablespoons butter or margarine
1 can (about 1 pound) tomatoes
$^1/_2$ cup water
2 tablespoons brown sugar
2 tablespoons vinegar
2 tablespoons Worcestershire sauce
1 teaspoon salt
1 teaspoon chili powder
1 teaspoon dry mustard
$^1/_2$ teaspoon celery seeds
1 clove garlic, minced
Few drops hot-pepper sauce

Not for timid palates, this highly sea-soned dish.

Makes 4 servings.

1. Dust drumsticks with seasoned flour.
2. Melt butter or margarine in large heavy frying pan with tight-fitting cover; brown chicken over medium heat on all sides; drain on absorbent paper.
3. Combine all remaining ingredients in same pan.
4. Bring to boil; reduce heat; return chicken to pan; cover.
5. Simmer chicken 40 to 45 minutes, or until tender.
6. Serve with pan sauce.

SKILLET CHICKEN AND VEGETABLES

You can start this meal-in-one well be-forehand and refrigerate it, then finish cooking it just before dinnertime.

Makes 6 servings.

6 drumsticks with thighs (about 3 pounds)
6 slices bacon, halved
$^1/_3$ cup flour
1 teaspoon salt
$^1/_4$ teaspoon pepper
2 cans (12 ounces each) Mexican-style
   corn
$^3/_4$ cup milk
2 packages (10 ounces each) frozen
   Fordhook lima beans
1 cup thinly sliced celery

1. Cut through chicken legs at joints to separate drumsticks and thighs; wash pieces and dry.
2. Sauté bacon until crisp in a large heavy frying pan; remove and drain on paper toweling. Wrap and chill until just before serving time.

3. Brown chicken pieces in bacon drippings in same pan; remove and set aside.
4. Stir flour, salt, and pepper into drippings; cook, stirring constantly, until bubbly. Drain liquid from corn into a small bowl; stir milk into corn liquid, then stir into flour mixture in frying pan. Continue cooking and stirring until gravy thickens and boils 1 minute. Return chicken, arranging pieces in a single layer; cover. Chill, along with corn.
5. An hour before serving, heat chicken and gravy very slowly to boiling; simmer 45 minutes; pile chicken in center of pan.
6. Pour boiling water to cover over limas and celery in a medium-size bowl; let stand 3 minutes, breaking up limas as they thaw; drain. Place at one side of chicken in pan; place corn at other side; cover. Simmer 10 minutes. Arrange bacon over chicken; continue cooking 5 minutes, or until beans are tender and bacon is heated through. Just before serving, garnish with parsley, if you wish.

CHICKEN WINGS

Chicken wings are small but flavory, and make delicious finger food to serve at parties. Remember to buy plenty — they have only morsels of meat on them. Here are three good ways to fix chicken wings.

BREADED CHICKEN WINGS

A batch of tasty tidbits for nibblers.

Bake at 350° for 1 hour.

3 pounds chicken wings (about 25)
¹/₂ cup vegetable oil
1 teaspoon seasoned salt
1¹/₂ cups corn-flake crumbs or bread crumbs

1. Trim tips from chicken wings; divide wings in half by cutting through remaining joints with a sharp knife.

2. Mix vegetable oil and seasoned salt in a pie plate; place corn-flake or bread crumbs in a second pie plate. Roll chicken pieces in oil mixture, then in crumbs to coat evenly. Place, not touching, in a large shallow pan.

3. Bake in moderate oven (350°) 1 hour, or until golden. Serve hot.

CHICKEN WINGS SESAME

These crisp morsels make a fine appetizer at dinner or main dish at luncheon.

2¹/₂ to 3 pounds chicken wings (20 to 25)
1 egg
¹/₂ cup milk
¹/₄ cup sesame seeds
¹/₂ cup flour
1 teaspoon salt
¹/₄ teaspoon pepper
¹/₄ teaspoon ground ginger
4 tablespoons butter or margarine

Bake at 350° for 1 to 1¹/₄ hours.

1. Wash chickens wings and pat dry.

2. Beat egg slightly in a bowl with milk.

3. In another bowl, combine sesame seeds, flour, salt, pepper, and ginger.

4. Melt butter in baking pan. Dip chicken wings in egg mixture, then in seed mixture, and place in baking pan, rolling them in butter to coat them.

5. Bake at 350° for 1 to 1¹/₄ hours or until brown, crisp, and fork-tender.

PICKUP CHICKEN STICKS

Luscious finger-food to serve at an open house, buffet lunch, or cocktail party.

Bake at 350° for 1 hour.

3 pounds chicken wings (about 25)
1 cup (2 sticks) butter or margarine
1¹/₂ cups sifted flour
¹/₃ cup finely crushed toasted almonds
1 tablespoon salt
¹/₂ teaspoon ground ginger

1. Singe chicken wings, if necessary; cut off and discard tips. Divide each wing in half by cutting through joint with a sharp knife. Wash and drain on paper toweling.

2. Melt butter or margarine in large shallow baking pan. Mix flour, crushed almonds, salt, and ginger in pie plate.

3. Roll chicken pieces, one at a time, in butter or margarine in pan, letting any excess drip back. Roll in flour mixture to coat generously, then set aside on waxed paper sheets until all are coated. Arrange, not touching, in single layer in same pan.

4. Bake in moderate oven (350°) 1 hour, or until tender and richly golden on bottom. Brown in broiler for 3 to 5 minutes.

Chicken-Liver-Tomato Kebabs

CHICKEN LIVERS

Delicate little chicken livers are considered heavenly by many people. One thing is sure — they cook quickly and are a boon to a cook-in-a-hurry. As the recipes on these pages show, chicken livers make fine kebabs; they combine well with eggs, bacon, or mushrooms; they can be fried in potato pancakes. And for a pâté and a spread with chicken livers, see the section on APPETIZERS.

CHICKEN-LIVER-TOMATO KEBABS

A light and pretty dish bound to boost a hostess' reputation.

Makes 4 servings.

12 chicken livers (about 1 pound)
4 slices bacon, halved
16 cherry tomatoes
2 tablespoons Worcestershire sauce

1. Halve chicken livers; snip out any veiny parts or skin with scissors.
2. Sauté bacon slices until partly cooked in a medium-size frying pan; remove and drain well on paper toweling. Wrap slices around 8 of the liver halves; hold in place with wooden picks, if needed.
3. Thread each of 8 long thin skewers this way: cherry tomato, plain chicken liver half, bacon-wrapped liver, plain liver half, and cherry tomato, allowing about ¼ inch between each. Place on rack in broiler pan; brush with part of the Worcestershire sauce.
4. Broil, 6 inches from heat, 7 minutes; turn. Brush with remaining Worcestershire sauce, then continue broiling 7 minutes, or until bacon is crisp. Remove wooden picks before serving.

Quick and Easy   ## LITTLE LIVERS SPECIALTY

Don't overcook these delicious tidbits.

Makes 4 servings.

1 pound chicken livers
¼ cup sifted flour
½ teaspoon salt
⅛ teaspoon pepper
2 tablespoons butter or margarine
1 can (3 or 4 ounces) sliced mushrooms
1½ teaspoons Worcestershire sauce

1. Shake chicken livers, a few at a time, in mixture of flour, salt, and pepper in paper bag to coat evenly.
2. Brown in butter or margarine in large heavy frying pan over low heat. Stir in mushrooms and liquid and Worcestershire sauce.
3. Cover loosely; cook slowly 10 minutes, or just until liquid is absorbed.

CHICKEN LIVERS STROGONOFF

Sour cream sauce turns these delicacies into a Continental dish.

Makes 6 servings.

1 pound chicken livers
2 tablespoons butter or margarine
$1/2$ teaspoon oregano
$1/2$ teaspoon Worcestershire sauce
1 medium-size onion, chopped ($1/2$ cup)
2 tablespoons flour
$1/2$ teaspoon salt
Dash of pepper
1 can (6 ounces) sliced mushrooms
$1/4$ cup dairy sour cream

1. Halve chicken livers; snip out any veiny parts or skin with scissors.
2. Brown livers slowly in butter or margarine seasoned with oregano and Worcestershire sauce; remove from pan. Add onion; sauté until soft.
3. Blend in flour, salt, and pepper; stir in mushrooms and liquid. Heat stirring constantly, to boiling; return livers; cover. Simmer 3 minutes, or just until livers lose their pink color.
4. Stir about ¼ cup liver mixture into sour cream, then stir back into remaining in pan. Heat very slowly just until hot. Serve over fluffy rice and garnish with crisp bacon slices, if you wish.

CHICKEN LIVER KNISHES

A traditional Jewish snack, these delicious liver-filled pancakes (pronounced ka-nishes) should please all palates.

Makes about 3 dozen.

$1^{1}/2$ pounds chicken livers
$1/4$ cup vegetable oil
3 large onions, sliced thin (3 cups)
3 teaspoons salt
10 large potatoes, pared and sliced thin
1 egg
$1^{1}/4$ cups matzo meal OR finely crushed
  unsalted cracker crumbs
Shortening or vegetable oil for frying

1. Sauté chicken livers, turning once, in the ¼ cup vegetable oil in a large frying pan 5 minutes, or just until they lose their pink color; lift out with a slotted spoon and place in a large bowl.
2. Stir onions into drippings in pan; sauté until soft; combine with livers. Put livers and onions through a food grinder, using a coarse blade; return to bowl. Stir in 1 teaspoon of the salt, chill.
3. Cook potatoes, covered, in boiling salted water in a large saucepan 15 minutes, or until tender; drain well. Mash, then beat in egg, remaining 2 teaspoons salt, and ¼ cup of the matzo meal; chill.
4. When ready to finish cakes, measure remaining 1 cup matzo meal into a pie plate. Place potato mixture, a heaping tablespoonful at a time, into matzo meal and flatten into a 4-inch round; place a heaping teaspoonful liver mixture in center. Shape potato round up and over filling to cover completely. Roll in matzo meal to coat lightly.
5. Melt enough shortening or pour vegetable oil into a large frying pan to make a depth of ⅛ inch. Add potato cakes, a few at a time, to hot fat and fry, turning once, 3 to 5 minutes, or until golden. (Add more shortening or oil and reheat between batches as needed.) Serve hot.

CHICKEN-LIVER-MUSHROOM KEBABS

An interesting variation on the popular kebab theme.

Makes 4 servings.

4 bacon strips, cut in quarters
12 small mushroom caps
12 chicken livers (about 1 pound)
2 tablespoons melted butter or margarine
Salt and pepper

1. On a 7-inch skewer, string a folded-over piece of bacon, a mushroom cap, and a chicken liver; repeat 2 more times, ending with bacon; repeat to fill 4 skewers.
2. Place in shallow baking pan; brush with melted butter or margarine.
3. Place in broiler with top of food 4 inches from unit or tip of flame, and broil 10 minutes, or until livers are cooked through and bacon is crisp, turning once and basting once or twice with drippings. Sprinkle with salt and pepper to taste.
4. Remove food from each skewer onto a hot plate and serve.

CHICKEN LIVERS WITH BACON CRISPS

Harmonious morsels, oven baked and served on toast.

Bake at 400° for 30 minutes.

Makes 6 servings.

12 slices (about ¹/₂ pound) bacon
1 pound chicken livers
4 tablespoons flour
1 teaspoon salt
¹/₂ teaspoon paprika
6 slices hot toast
Pepper

1. Lay bacon slices in single layer on rack of broiler pan. (If slices don't separate easily, heat in oven for a few minutes.) Bake in hot oven (400°) 10 minutes, or until crisp. (No need to turn.) Remove rack with bacon on it; keep warm. (Leave oven heat on.)
2. Shake chicken livers in mixture of flour, salt, and paprika in paper bag to coat well; lay in hot drippings in broiler pan.
3. Bake in hot oven (400°) 10 minutes, or until browned on underside; turn; bake 10 minutes longer, or until browned on other side. Drain on paper toweling.
4. Arrange toast slices in single layer on heated large serving platter; brush very lightly with bacon drippings from broiler pan. Arrange livers on top; sprinkle with pepper; top with criss-crossed bacon slices.

Quick and Easy   CHICKEN LIVERS AND EGGS

A perfect dish to whip up for brunch, light supper, or midnight snack.

Makes 4 servings.

6 eggs
6 tablespoons milk
³/₄ teaspoon salt
Dash of pepper
¹/₂ pound chicken livers OR 1 package (8 ounces) frozen chicken livers, thawed
Salt and pepper
2 teaspoons butter or margarine

1. Combine eggs, milk, salt, and pepper in medium-size bowl; beat until foamy; save for Step 4.
2. Cut chicken livers into small pieces; sprinkle with salt and pepper.
3. Melt butter or margarine in medium-size frying pan; fry livers over medium heat, stirring several times, 3 to 4 minutes, or until lightly browned.
4. Add milk-egg mixture; cook over low heat, stirring several times, 3 to 4 minutes, or until eggs are set.

125

Chilled Chicken Cream

CHICKEN SOUPS

Besides all its other virtues, chicken makes luscious soups. Chicken soups can be hot or cold, creamy or clear, thin or hearty. Take your pick among these; some are start-from-scratch, others are based on canned soups. And for a truly exotic chicken soup, turn to Tobago Chicken-Avocado Soup in CHICKEN SOUTH-OF-THE-BORDER.

CHUNKY CHICKEN-BEEF SOUP

An entire broiler-fryer and plenty of beef go into this made-from-scratch soup.

Makes 8 servings.

1¹/₂ **pounds chuck beefsteak, cut into ¹/₂ inch cubes**
1 **large onion, chopped (1 cup)**
1 **broiler-fryer, weighing 2¹/₂ to 3 pounds, quartered**
1 **cup chopped celery**
2 **teaspoons salt**
1 **teaspoon seasoned salt**
¹/₂ **teaspoon pepper**
¹/₂ **teaspoon leaf rosemary, crumbled**
¹/₂ **teaspoon leaf thyme, crumbled**
1 **bay leaf**
10 **cups water**
2 **cups uncooked medium noodles**

1. Brown beef in its own fat in a kettle or Dutch oven; stir in onion and sauté lightly.
2. Add chicken, celery, salt, seasoned salt, pepper, rosemary, thyme, bay leaf, and water to kettle; heat to boiling; cover. Simmer 1 hour, or until chicken is tender; remove from kettle. Continue cooking beef 20 minutes, or until tender; remove bay leaf.
3. While beef finishes cooking, pull skin from chicken and take meat from bones; cut meat into cubes. Return to kettle; heat to boiling.
4. Stir in noodles. Cook 10 minutes, or until noodles are tender.
5. Ladle into soup plates. Sprinkle with chopped parsley and serve with your favorite crisp crackers, if you wish.

127

CHICKEN-CUCUMBER SOUP

This pale and pretty soup is an American version of a Japanese favorite.

Makes 6 servings.

6 cups canned clear chicken bouillon
3 teaspoons soy sauce (more or less, to suit taste)
3 teaspoons lemon juice (more or less, to suit taste)
Dash of monosodium glutamate
2 cucumbers, peeled and diced
6 eggs

1. Heat bouillon and add soy sauce and lemon juice, according to taste. Season to taste with monosodium glutamate. Heat to boiling.
2. Add diced cucumber and simmer 4 or 5 minutes.
3. Lift out cucumbers and divide among 6 soup bowls. Keep warm.
4. Poach eggs in the hot bouillon. When done, lift an egg into each soup bowl. Ladle bouillon into bowls, and serve hot.

MAMA'S CHICKEN-NOODLE SOUP

Here's the famous Jewish soup that traditionalists recommend to cure all ills — and even mend broken hearts.

Makes 8 servings.

1 stewing chicken (about 5 pounds)
2 medium-size carrots, pared and sliced
1 large stalk celery, trimmed and chopped
1 large onion, sliced
3 teaspoons salt
1/4 teaspoon pepper
10 cups water
2 cups fine noodles

1. Rinse inside of chicken well with cold water. Place in a kettle; add carrots, celery, onion, salt, pepper, and the 10 cups water; heat to boiling; cover.
2. Simmer 2 hours, or until chicken is tender. Remove from broth; cool until easy to handle, then take meat from bones and chill to use another day.
3. Let broth stand until fat rises to top, then skim off. Reheat broth to boiling, stir in noodles. Cook 10 minutes, or until noodles are tender.
4. Ladle soup into heated bowls or soup plates; sprinkle with chopped parsley.

CHICKEN-CORN CHOWDER

Canned chicken soup, canned corn, canned milk — by the time the kids wash up, soup's on!

Makes 6 servings.

1 medium-size onion, chopped (1/2 cup)
2 tablespoons butter or margarine
2 cans condensed chicken noodle soup
1 soup can water
1 can (about 1 pound) cream-style corn
1 small can evaporated milk (2/3 cup)
1/4 teaspoon pepper
2 tablespoons chopped parsley

1. Sauté onion in butter or margarine just until soft in medium-size saucepan.
2. Stir in remaining ingredients, except parsley. Heat just to boiling.
3. Pour into heated soup bowls or mugs; sprinkle with parsley.

COLD SENEGALESE SOUP

Midsummer's dream: a cold and simple gourmet dish.

Makes 6 servings.

1 can condensed cream of chicken soup
1 tall can evaporated milk
1 tablespoon lemon juice
1 teaspoon curry powder

1. Combine all ingredients in large bowl; beat (or blend in an electric blender) until creamy-smooth; chill.
2. Serve in cups or bowls. If you like, sprinkle with chopped toasted almonds or flaked coconut.

HOT SENEGALESE SOUP

This creamy soup is an exotic but very easy version of an honored specialty.

Makes 8 servings.

2 cans condensed cream of chicken soup
3 cups milk
1/2 teaspoon curry powder
2 tablespoons toasted coconut

1. Combine soup, milk, and curry powder in medium-size saucepan; heat just until bubbly-hot, then beat with rotary beater until creamy smooth.
2. Pour into 8 small bowls or cups, dividing evenly; sprinkle with coconut.

CHILLED CHICKEN CREAM

Celery seeds give canned cream soup an exceptional flavor.

Makes 6 servings.

1 can condensed cream of chicken soup
1 cup light or table cream
1/2 cup milk
1 teaspoon lemon juice
1/2 teaspoon celery seeds

1. Combine all ingredients in an electric-blender container; cover. Blend 1 minute, or until creamy smooth. (Or beat slightly longer with an electric beater.) Chill.
2. Pour into mugs or cups. Garnish each with a celery-stick stirrer and serve with tiny croutons to sprinkle over, or a dash of paprika, if you wish.

CHICKEN-LEMON SOUP

Here's a cool and tangy opener for a warm-weather supper.

Makes 4 to 6 servings.

1 enevlope chicken-noodle soup mix
1 cup thinly sliced celery
4 teaspoons lemon juice
2 hard-cooked eggs, finely diced

1. Prepare soup mix, following label directions; cook 5 minutes; add celery and cook 2 minutes longer.
2. Remove from heat; stir in lemon juice; pour into bowl; cover; chill.
3. Serve in cups or small bowls, with diced hard-cooked eggs sprinkled over.

APPETIZERS, PATES, DIPS

Because of its ability to play so many roles in company with so many other foods — and seasonings — chicken can be the basis of many pre-dinner dishes. It turns up with eggs, mushrooms, ham, shrimp, cheese, sour cream, and just about all the herbs and spices on earth. Some of the appetizer recipes here begin with uncooked chicken; some are based on canned chicken, broth, or spread. For more party or first-course snacks, see CHICKEN WINGS, the Chinese Chicken Egg Rolls in ORIENTAL CHICKEN, and the Chicken Liver Knishes in LIVERS.

CHICKEN AND SHRIMPS MARENGO

For favorite guests — here's a festive appetizer, served in a chafing dish, warmer, or scallop shells.

Makes 8 servings.

1 chicken breast (about 12 ounces)
4 tablespoons vegetable oil
1/2 teaspoon monosodium glutamate
1 large onion, chopped (1 cup)
1 clove garlic, minced
2 tablespoons flour
1 can (2 1/4 ounces) deviled ham
1 can (8 ounces) stewed tomatoes
1 can (3 or 4 ounces) whole mushrooms
1 teaspoon Worcestershire sauce
1 pound fresh shrimps, shelled and
   deveined
Chopped parsley

1. Pull skin from chicken breast; cut meat from bones in two large pieces, then cut into 1-inch pieces.
2. Brown in 2 tablespoons of the vegetable oil in a medium-size frying pan; sprinkle with monosodium glutamate; cover. Cook slowly 15 minutes, or until tender.
3. While chicken cooks, sauté onion and garlic until soft in remaining 2 tablespoons vegetable oil in a second medium-size frying pan; blend in flour; cook, stirring constantly, until bubbly.
4. Blend in deviled ham, then stir in tomatoes, mushrooms and their liquid, and Worcestershire sauce. Cook, stirring constantly, until mixture thickens and boils 1 minute; remove chicken from its frying pan with a slotted spoon and stir into sauce.
5. Stir shrimps into chicken drippings in frying pan; cook slowly, turning once, 10 minutes, or until tender. Stir into sauce mixture.
6. Spoon into scallop shells, a chafing dish, or a keep-hot server; sprinkle with chopped parsley. Serve with small triangles of crisp toast, if you wish.

PATE CONTINENTAL

It's a lot of work and must be made well ahead, but the result is a beautiful pâté loaf to grace a party table.

Bake at 350° for 1½ hours.

Makes 8 servings.

1 pound beef liver
½ pound chicken livers
1 medium-size onion, chopped (½ cup)
2 tablespoons butter or margarine
¼ cup water
1 envelope instant chicken broth OR
    1 chicken bouillon cube
2 eggs, beaten
¼ teaspoon ground allspice
¼ teaspoon leaf thyme, crumbled
5 slices bacon
Beef Aspic
1 hard-cooked egg, shelled

1. Snip out any large tubelike membranes from beef liver; cut into chunks. Halve chicken livers; snip out any veiny parts or skin.
2. Put both meats through a food chopper, using a fine blade; place in a medium-size bowl.
3. Sauté onion in butter or margarine until soft in a small frying pan; stir in water and chicken broth or bouillon cube; heat to boiling, crushing bouillon cube, if used, with a spoon; stir into liver mixture with eggs, allspice, and thyme.
4. Place 3 slices of the bacon in a loaf pan, 5x3x2; spoon in liver mixture; top with remaining bacon. Cover pan tightly with foil.
5. Set in baking pan on oven shelf; pour boiling water into pan to depth of about 1 inch.
6. Bake in moderate oven (350°) 1½ hours, or until loaf starts to pull away from sides of pan; remove from pan of water; take off foil. Cool loaf, then chill overnight.

7. Make Beef Aspic.
8. Peel bacon from top of loaf; loosen loaf around edges with a knife; invert onto a plate; peel off remaining bacon. Wash pan and dry well.
9. Pour ¼ cup of the aspic into loaf pan; place in a pan of ice and water to speed setting; chill just until sticky-firm.
10. While layer chills, halve hard-cooked egg lengthwise, cutting just through the white. Slice yolk carefully; cut white into 8 or 10 tiny flower shapes with a truffle cutter. Arrange two of the egg-yolk slices and egg-white cut-outs in a pretty pattern on sticky-firm aspic in pan; carefully pour in another ½ cup aspic; let set until sticky-firm.
11. Place pâté loaf over aspic layer in pan; pour in enough of the remaining aspic to fill pan to rim. Remove from ice and water; chill in refrigerator at least 4 hours, or until aspic is firm. Pour remaining aspic into a pan, 8x8x2; chill.
12. Just before serving, run a sharp-tip thin-blade knife around top of loaf, then dip pan *very quickly* in and out of hot water. Cover pan with a chilled serving plate; turn upside down; gently lift off pan.
13. Cut remaining aspic layer into tiny cubes; spoon around pâté loaf. Garnish with radish flowers and snips of radish leaves, if you wish.
  To make radish flowers, trim large radishes. Holding each, tip end up, cut lengthwise into 10 or 12 sections, cutting not quite to stem. Place in a bowl of ice and water until "petals" open up.

BEEF ASPIC: Soften 1 envelope unflavored gelatin in ¾ cup cold water in a small saucepan; heat, stirring constantly, just until gelatin dissolves; remove from heat. Stir in 1 can condensed beef consommé and 2 tablespoons lemon juice. Cool.

CHICKEN CANAPES

Flavory salad is heaped into tiny pastry shells and topped with a miniature tomato slice.

Makes 5 dozen, or about 25 servings.

Canapé Shells
1 can (6 ounces) chopped broiled mushrooms
2 cans (5 to 6 ounces each) boned chicken, very finely chopped OR 2 cups very finely chopped cooked chicken
1/2 cup very finely diced celery
2/3 cup dairy sour cream
1 teaspoon grated onion
1/2 teaspoon curry powder
1/2 teaspoon salt
Cherry tomatoes, sliced
Parsley

1. Make, bake, and cool Canapé Shells.
2. Drain and chop mushrooms very fine. Combine with chicken and celery in a medium-size bowl.
3. Mix sour cream, onion, curry powder, and salt in a 1-cup measure; spoon over chicken mixture; toss well to mix; chill.

4. Just before serving, spoon into Canapé Shells, using 1 rounded teaspoonful for each. Garnish with a slice of cherry tomato and a sprig of parsley.

CANAPE SHELLS: Prepare 1 package pie-crust mix, following label directions, or make pastry from your own favorite two-crust recipe. Roll out, half at a time, to a 12-inch round on lightly floured pastry cloth or board; cut into small rounds with a 1¾-inch scalloped cutter. Fit into tiny muffin-pan cups; prick shells with a fork. Reroll and cut out all trimmings. Bake in hot oven (425°) 7 minutes, or until delicately golden. Remove from cups; cool completely on wire racks. Makes about 5 dozen.

MAKE-AHEAD NOTE: Canapé Shells may be made a day ahead, if you like, then stacked and stored in a container with a tight-fitting cover. For 100 servings, make 3 times the recipe. For variety, fill with your favorite seafood or ham salad.

Quick and Easy   PIMIENTO CHICKEN LIVER SPREAD

A nippy, colorful canapé spread you can whip up in a flash.

Makes about ¾ cup.

1 can or jar (2 ounces) pimientos, chopped
1/2 cup chopped, cooked chicken livers
2 hard-cooked eggs, diced
1 teaspoon chopped onion
1 teaspoon prepared mustard
Dash Worcestershire sauce
Mayonnaise or cream to moisten
Sprigs of parsley for garnish

1. Blend all ingredients.
2. Spread on crisp crackers or toasted rounds of bread. Garnish each canapé with sprig of parsley.

PATE-CHEESE MOLD

Stuffed olives crown a pretty double-molded spread of meat and cheese.

Makes 25 servings.

MEAT LAYER

1 envelope unflavored gelatin
1 envelope instant chicken broth OR
   1 chicken bouillon cube
1 cup water
1 tablespoon lemon juice
3 large stuffed green olives, sliced
1/2 pound bologna
1/4 cup mayonnaise or salad dressing
1/4 cup sweet mustard relish (from a 9-ounce jar)

CHEESE LAYER

1 envelope unflavored gelatin
1/4 cup water
2 wedges (1 1/3 ounces each) Camembert cheese
1/4 pound blue cheese
1/4 teaspoon curry powder
1 egg, separated
1 cup (8-ounce carton) dairy sour cream
Green food coloring

1. Make meat layer: Soften gelatin with chicken broth or bouillon cube in water in a small saucepan. Heat, stirring constantly and crushing cube, if using, with a spoon, just until gelatin dissolves. Measure 1/4 cup into a 6-cup mold; stir in lemon juice. (Keep remaining gelatin mixture at room temperature.)
2. Set mold in a pan of ice and water to speed setting; chill just until syrupy-thick.

Arrange stuffed olive slices in gelatin to make a pretty pattern. Chill until sticky-firm.
3. While mold chills, remove skin from bologna; put meat through a food chopper, using a fine blade. Mix with remaining gelatin mixture, mayonnaise or salad dressing, and relish in a medium-size bowl; spoon over sticky-firm olive layer in mold. Continue chilling in same pan of ice and water until sticky-firm while making cheese layer.
4. Make cheese layer: Soften gelatin in water in a small saucepan; heat slowly just until gelatin dissolves.
5. Beat Camembert and blue cheeses until well-blended in a medium-size bowl; beat in curry powder, egg yolk, and dissolved gelatin.
6. Beat egg white until it stands in firm peaks in a small bowl. Fold into cheese mixture, then fold in sour cream. Tint mixture light green with a drop or two of food coloring.
7. Spoon over sticky-firm meat layer in mold; cover with waxed paper, foil, or transparent wrap. Chill in refrigerator several hours, or until firm. (Overnight is best.)
8. When ready to unmold, run a sharp-tip, thin-blade knife around top of mold, then dip mold very quickly in and out of a pan of hot water. Cover mold with a serving plate; turn upside down; gently lift off mold. Surround with your choice of crisp crackers.

CHICKEN TANGO DIP

The secret ingredient (instant coffee) makes this a delicious, mellow dip.

Makes 2 cups.

1 can (5 ounces) chicken spread
1 cup (8-ounce carton) dairy sour cream
1/4 cup mayonnaise or salad dressing
1/4 cup finely chopped walnuts
2 teaspoons instant coffee
1/4 teaspoon salt
Dash of pepper
1 teaspoon lemon juice

1. Combine all ingredients in a medium-size bowl; stir lightly until well blended. Chill several hours to season.
2. Spoon into small bowls; sprinkle with paprika, if you wish. Serve with crisp green-pepper squares, carrot sticks, potato chips, pretzels, or your favorite crackers.

CHICKEN ROLLS

A first-rate first course, or party fare: crisp gingery rolls of white meat and ham.

Makes 6 servings (3 rolls each).

1 whole chicken breast (about 12 ounces)
2 slices boiled ham, each cut into 9 pieces
18 small thin strips crystallized ginger
1 egg
1/4 cup milk
1/2 cup sifted regular flour
1/2 teaspoon salt
1/2 teaspoon sugar
Shortening or vegetable oil for frying

1. Pull skin from chicken breast; halve breast and cut meat in 1 piece from bone, then cut each half into 9 even pieces. Place, 2 or 3 at a time, between waxed paper and pound very thin with mallet or rolling pin until about 2 inches wide.
2. Top each with a piece of ham and ginger; roll up. Place, seam side down, in a single layer on a large platter; cover; chill.

3. When ready to cook, beat egg with milk in a medium-size bowl; beat in flour, salt, and sugar until smooth. (Batter will be medium-thin.)
4. Melt enough shortening or pour in enough vegetable oil to make a 4-inch depth in an electric deep-fat fryer or large saucepan; heat to 380°.
5. Dip chicken rolls, 2 or 3 at a time, into batter; hold over bowl to let excess drip back.
6. Fry in hot shortening, turning once, 3 minutes, or until golden; lift out with a slotted spoon; drain on paper toweling. Serve hot with dips of prepared horseradish-mustard and Plum Sauce (see section on SAUCES), if you wish.

MAKE-AHEAD TIP: Rolls may be fried several hours ahead and chilled. To reheat, arrange, not touching, in a shallow baking pan and heat in very hot oven (450°) 10 minutes.

PATE MIMOSA

This pearly chicken-flavored mold includes little nuggets of bacon and hard-cooked eggs.

Makes 12 servings.

1 envelops unflavored gelatin
1 envelope instant chicken broth
1½ cups water
½ cup mayonnaise or salad dressing
2 teaspoons cider vinegar
1 teaspoon grated onion
1 teaspoon prepared horseradish
1 teaspoon salt
⅛ teaspoon cayenne pepper
6 slices crisp bacon, crumbled
4 hard-cooked eggs, shelled and sieved

1. Combine gelatin, chicken broth, and water in a small saucepan; heat, stirring constantly, until gelatin dissolves.

2. Beat in mayonnaise or salad dressing, vinegar, onion, horseradish, salt, and cayenne pepper. Pour into a shallow pan; chill in freezer 20 minutes, or just until firm at edges.

3. Spoon into a bowl; beat until fluffy. Fold in bacon and eggs; spoon into a 3-cup mold. Chill until firm.

4. Unmold onto a serving plate; frame with toast rounds, if you wish.

5. Crown mold with a wreath of sieved hard-cooked egg yolk, outlined with tufts of parsley.

CHICKEN
SANDWICHES

Chicken sandwiches know no season and taste as good hot as they do cold. Even sliced chicken unadorned between two pieces of buttered toast can taste good. The sandwich recipes here offer a bit more than that, with two chicken salad rolls, two clubs, one hot chicken liver mixture, and one chicken-with-mushroom spread. For sandwiches especially good for picnics, see Chicken Jumbos and Chicken Double-Deckers, in the PICNIC CHICK section.

STUFFED SALAD ROLLS

2 cups chopped lettuce
1 cup diced cooked chicken
¹/₂ cup diced process American or
  Swiss cheese
¹/₂ cup chopped celery
¹/₂ cup mayonnaise
2 tablespoons pickle relish
¹/₄ teaspoon curry powder
8 frankfurter rolls, split, toasted, and
  buttered

A tasty jumble of chopped chicken, cheese, and celery, piled on frankfurter rolls. Makes 4 servings, 2 rolls each.

1. Combine lettuce with chicken, cheese, and celery in medium-size bowl.
2. Blend mayonnaise, pickle relish, and curry powder in small bowl; stir into salad mixture to coat well; pile into prepared rolls.

CHICKEN-MUSHROOM SPREAD SPECIALS

3 tablespoons butter or margarine
1 tablespoon minced onion
2 tablespoons flour
¹/₂ cup milk
4 tablespoons grated Parmesan cheese
1 cup ground up cooked chicken
1 cup fresh mushrooms, minced, OR 1 cup
  canned mushroom stems and pieces,
  minced and drained
Salt and pepper
6 slices buttered toast

Serve these open-face sandwiches hot, for luncheon or for appetizers. Makes 6 luncheon sandwiches or 24 appetizers.

1. Melt butter or margarine in large skillet and add minced onion; fry until tender.
2. Blend in flour; gradually add milk and 2 tablespoons grated cheese.
3. Stir in chicken and mushrooms. Season to taste with salt and pepper.
4. Spread on buttered toast and sprinkle with remaining 2 tablespoons Parmesan cheese. (If serving as appetizers, cut each piece of toast into quarters.) Serve hot.

CHICKEN CHEESE CLUBS

Chicken, bacon, and Muenster — a flavory combo — spiked with tomatoes and cucumber.

Bake at 450° for 5 minutes.

Makes 4 sandwiches.

12 slices bacon (¹/₂ pound)
2 medium-size tomatoes, each cut in
** 4 slices**
¹/₂ small cucumber, sliced
12 slices whole-wheat bread, toasted
** and buttered**
¹/₄ cup prepared sandwich spread
8 slices cooked chicken
4 slices Muenster cheese (from an 8-ounce
** package)**
8 pitted ripe olives
8 small sweet pickles

1. Sauté bacon until crisp in a large frying pan; drain on paper toweling.
2. Place tomato and cucumber slices and bacon, dividing evenly, on 4 pieces of the toast; add another slice of the toast; spread with sandwich spread.

3. Top with chicken slices, then cheese and remaining toast, buttered side down. Place sandwiches on a cooky sheet.
4. Bake in a very hot oven (450°) 5 minutes, or until cheese melts slightly.
5. Press wooden picks into sandwiches to hold in place; cut each sandwich diagonally into quarters. Top picks with olives and pickles.

CHICKEN LIVER BOUNTIES

Here's a sandwich to please gourmets. Cook the livers gently, then combine with broiled tomatoes and crisp bacon.

Makes 6 sandwiches.

6 slices bacon
1 pound chicken livers
2 tablespoons flour
¹/₄ teaspoon seasoned salt
1 can (3 or 4 ounces) chopped mushrooms
3 large tomatoes, each cut in 6 slices
3 large hamburger buns, split

1. Sauté bacon just until crisp in a large frying pan; drain on paper toweling, then crumble. Drain off all drippings, then measure 2 tablespoons and return to pan. (Set bacon aside for Step 5.)
2. Halve chicken livers; snip out any veiny

parts or skin with scissors. Shake livers with flour and seasoned salt in a paper bag to coat.
3. Brown slowly in drippings in frying pan; stir in mushrooms and liquid. Heat, stirring constantly, to boiling; cover. Simmer 3 minutes, or just until livers lose their pink color.
4. While livers cook, place tomato slices and bun halves in a single layer on rack in broiler pan. Broil 3 to 4 minutes, or until tomatoes are heated through and buns are toasted.
5. Place 2 tomato slices on each bun half; spoon hot liver mixture over, dividing evenly. Top each with another tomato slice; sprinkle with crumbled bacon. Garnish with parsley, if you wish.

SHORT-CUT CLUBS

Chicken salad and deviled ham make up this quickie version of a popular sandwich.

Makes 4 servings.

1 cup diced cooked chicken
1 cup finely diced celery
¼ teaspoon salt
Dash of pepper
2 tablespoons mayonnaise or salad
  dressing
12 slices white bread, toasted and buttered
1 can (4½ ounces) deviled ham
2 medium-size tomatoes, sliced thin
Lettuce

1. Combine chicken, celery, salt, pepper, mayonnaise or salad dressing in small bowl; toss lightly to mix. (Fix chicken salad ahead, if you like, then cover and chill until ready to make sandwiches.)
2. Spread toast with deviled ham, then layer each of four slices this way: Chicken salad, toast, tomato slices, and lettuce; top with remaining toast, deviled ham side down. Hold in place with wooden picks.
3. Cut each in quarters; garnish with ripe or green olives, if you wish.

CALIFORNIA BUNWICHES

Elaborate chicken salad — the works — heaped on Vienna rolls.

Makes 6 servings.

2 whole chicken breasts (about 1½
  pounds)
2 cups water
1 medium-size onion, sliced
Handful of celery tops
1¼ teaspoons salt
3 peppercorns
1 can (14 ounces) pineapple tidbits,
  drained
1 cup diced celery
½ cup slivered almonds
½ cup mayonnaise
2 tablespoons milk
¼ teaspoon dry mustard
⅛ teaspoon pepper
6 Vienna rolls, split and buttered
Lettuce
Cherry tomatoes

1. Combine chicken breasts, water, onion, celery tops, 1 teaspoon salt, and peppercorns in large saucepan. Simmer, covered, 20 to 30 minutes, or until chicken is tender. Let stand until cool enough to handle, then skin chicken and take meat from bones. Dice chicken (you should have about 2 cups).
2. Combine chicken, pineapple, celery, and almonds in medium-size bowl. Mix mayonnaise, milk, ¼ teaspoon salt, mustard, and pepper in 1-cup measure; stir into chicken mixture, tossing lightly to mix; chill until serving time.
3. Line buttered rolls with lettuce; fill with salad mixture, dividing evenly. Top each with 2 or 3 cherry tomatoes.

LEFTOVER CHICKEN

A clever homemaker knows that the remains of yesterday's broiled, roast, baked, or boiled chicken can be the basis of a new, delicious dish. (A can or two of boned chicken can fill in where it's needed.) Only thing to remember is that if you are using leftovers from a strongly flavored chicken dish, the chicken will have a taste of its own to be considered in the new dish. This may be a good thing — it can even enhance the new concoction. Here are four hot and three cold dishes you can make with cooked chicken; for additional recipes turn to the SALADS and SANDWICHES sections. Or you might try Chicken Tetrazzini or Florentine Chicken in CONTINENTAL CHICKEN; Elegant Chicken with Cashews in COMPANY'S COMING; or the Chinese Egg Rolls in ORIENTAL CHICKEN.

PAGODA CHICKEN BOWL

Here is a delightful cold version of popular chicken and noodles.

Makes 4 servings.

1 package (6 ounces) noodles with chicken sauce mix and almonds
1 can (about 9 ounces) pineapple tidbits, drained
1 cup sliced celery
2 cups cubed, cooked chicken OR 2 cans (5 or 6 ounces) diced cooked chicken
1/3 cup mayonnaise or salad dressing
1/4 cup milk
1/4 teaspoon curry powder
Boston lettuce
Radish slices

1. Prepare noodles with chicken sauce mix, following label directions for top-range method; set almonds aside for Step 3. Spoon noodle mixture into a medium-size bowl; cool, stirring lightly several times at room temperature.
2. Set aside several pineapple tidbits and celery slices for a garnish; stir remaining with chicken into noodle mixture. Blend mayonnaise or salad dressing, milk, and curry powder in a cup; fold into noodle mixture. Chill at least 30 minutes to season.
3. When ready to serve, spoon into a lettuce-lined salad bowl; sprinkle with saved almonds on top. Garnish with rows of radish slices, and saved pineapple and celery threaded onto a wooden pick.

Quick and Easy

CHICKEN A LA KING

Nobody remembers what king this creamy dish is named for, but people have loved it since time immemorial.

Makes 4 servings.

4 tablespoons (¹/₂ stick) butter or margarine
¹/₄ cup flour
2 tablespoons finely chopped onion
1 teaspoon salt
¹/₂ teaspoon Worcestershire sauce
2 cups milk
2 cups diced cooked chicken OR 2 cans (5 or 6 ounces each) boned chicken, diced
¹/₄ cup diced pimiento (about 2 pimientos)
1 can (3 or 4 ounces) sliced mushrooms

1. Melt butter or margarine in medium-size saucepan; remove from heat.
2. Blend in flour, onion, salt, and Worcestershire sauce; stir in milk.
3. Cook over low heat, stirring constantly, until sauce thickens and boils 1 minute.
4. Stir in chicken, pimiento, and mushrooms; heat through.
5. Serve over hot buttered rice or toast, if desired.

CHICKEN CROQUETTES

When you go to a little trouble with left-over meat, it becomes a whole new dish.

Makes 8 croquettes.

2 cups coarsely ground cooked chicken
1 cup (about 2 slices) soft bread crumbs
2 eggs, well beaten
2 tablespoons plus ¹/₂ cup milk
1 tablespoon minced onion
1 tablespoon minced green pepper
¹/₂ teaspoon salt
¹/₄ teaspoon savory
Dash of pepper
¹/₄ cup finely chopped, blanched, toasted almonds
¹/₂ cup fine dry bread crumbs
Melted shortening, lard, or salad oil to make a 3-inch depth in kettle
Velouté Sauce

1. Combine chicken, soft bread crumbs, eggs, 2 tablespoons milk, onion, green pepper, salt, savory, pepper, and almonds in medium-size bowl; chill about 2 hours.
2. Shape into 8 cylindrical croquettes, each 1 inch in diameter; roll in fine dry bread crumbs; dip in ½ cup milk; roll again in crumbs; brush off loose crumbs.

3. Heat fat in deep heavy kettle to 365° or 375° (a 1-inch cube of bread will brown in about 1 minute).
4. Fry croquettes, 2 or 3 at a time, 2 minutes, or until golden-brown; drain on absorbent paper.
5. Serve on heated platter with Velouté Sauce.

VELOUTE SAUCE

Makes 2 cups sauce.

¹/₄ cup (¹/₂ stick) butter or margarine
¹/₄ cup sifted flour
¹/₈ teaspoon pepper
1 can chicken consommé
¹/₄ cup water
1 teaspoon lemon juice

1. Melt butter or margarine in small saucepan; remove from heat.
2. Blend in flour and pepper; gradually stir in consommé and water.
3. Cook over low heat, stirring constantly, until sauce thickens and boils 1 minute; stir in lemon juice. Serve hot.

CHICKEN-FRANKFURTER JAMBALAYA

This version of a Southern specialty goes from skillet to table in about 40 minutes.

Makes 6 servings.

8 frankfurters, sliced ¼ inch thick
1½ cups uncooked rice
2 tablespoons butter or margarine
2 cans (about 1 pound each) stewed tomatoes
1½ cups water
1½ teaspoons garlic salt
2 cups diced cooked chicken OR 2 cans (5 or 6 ounces each) boned chicken, diced
¼ cup diced green pepper

1. Sauté frankfurters and rice in butter or margarine in a large frying pan, stirring often, until rice is golden.
2. Stir in tomatoes, water, and garlic salt; place chicken on top; cover.
3. Simmer, stirring once, 30 minutes, or until rice is tender and liquid is absorbed.
4. Spoon into serving bowl; sprinkle with green pepper.

CHICKEN SLICES WITH SUPREME SAUCE

Tasty sauce goes over slices of cooked chicken in two layers; then you can pop the whole thing under the broiler to puff and brown.

Makes 4 servings.

4 servings of sliced cooked chicken
Supreme Sauce

1. Arrange chicken slices on broilerproof platter.
2. Spoon Supreme Sauce over in two layers as directed in sauce recipe.
3. Broil, about 4 inches from flame, 3 to 5 minutes, or until sauce puffs and browns. Serve at once.

SUPREME SAUCE

Makes about 2½ cups.

1 tablespoon finely chopped onion
5 tablespoons butter or margarine
5 tablespoons flour
½ teaspoon salt
⅛ teaspoon pepper
1 chicken bouillon cube
2 cups milk
4 tablespoons grated Parmesan cheese
2 tablespoons cream for whipping

1. Sauté onion in butter or margarine just until soft in a small heavy saucepan; stir in flour, salt, and pepper; cook, stirring all the time, over low heat, just until mixture bubbles; add bouillon cube.
2. Stir in milk slowly; continue cooking and stirring until bouillon cube dissolves and sauce thickens and boils 1 minute. Stir in 2 tablespoons of the cheese. (Set remaining cheese aside for Step 4.)
3. Measure out ½ cup sauce and set aside for next step; spoon remaining over chicken slices on platter.
4. Beat cream until stiff in a small bowl; fold into saved ½ cup sauce; spoon over first layer of sauce on chicken slices. Sprinkle with saved 2 tablespoons of Parmesan cheese.

CURRIED CHICKEN LEFTOVER

This one is a whole meal in itself. Almonds and apple add texture.

Makes 4 servings.

³/₄ cup precooked rice
¹/₂ cup chopped red apple
1 cup diced cooked chicken OR 1 can (5 or 6 ounces) boned chicken, diced
¹/₄ cup toasted slivered almonds
1¹/₂ teaspoons grated onion
¹/₃ cup mayonnaise or salad dressing
2 tablespoons cream
1 tablespoon lemon juice
¹/₂ teaspoon curry powder
¹/₄ teaspoon salt
¹/₄ teaspoon sugar

1. Cook rice in a small saucepan, following label directions; cool to room temperature. Combine with apple, chicken, almonds, onion in a medium-size bowl.
2. Blend remaining ingredients in a cup; stir into rice mixture; chill. Just before serving, garnish with red apple slices, if you wish.

DOUBLE SALAD JUMBO

Luscious for luncheon: seasoned asparagus and carrots and crunchy chicken salad, perched on golden waffles.

Makes 6 servings.

2 cups diced cooked chicken OR 2 cans (5 or 6 ounces each) boned chicken, diced
1¹/₂ cups diced celery
1 tablespoon chopped parsley
¹/₂ teaspoon seasoned salt
¹/₄ cup mayonnaise or salad dressing
1 can (1 pound) sliced carrots, drained
1 can (about 15 ounces) asparagus spears, drained
3 tablespoons bottled thin French dressing
12 frozen waffles
Boston lettuce
Pretzel sticks

1. Combine chicken with celery, parsley, and seasoned salt in a medium-size bowl; fold in mayonnaise or salad dressing. Chill at least 30 minutes to season and blend flavors.
2. Place carrots and asparagus in separate piles in a shallow dish; drizzle French dressing over all. Chill at least 30 minutes to season.
3. Just before serving, toast waffles, following label directions; place 2 on each of 6 serving plates; top each with several leaves of lettuce.
4. Spoon ½ cup chicken salad on one waffle on each plate; arrange carrots and asparagus in bundles on remaining waffles. Garnish each plate generously with pretzel sticks.

STUFFINGS

Where roast chicken is concerned, it is the stuffing that really makes the dish. The stuffing can be a simple bread-crumb mixture, moistened with butter and lightly seasoned, or it can be a glorious concoction of fruits and nuts. When you choose roast chicken as your main dish, suit your stuffing to the rest of the meal.

See also the step-by-step directions, HOW TO STUFF AND TRUSS CHICKEN. But cook your chicken as soon as you have stuffed it — it will ruin the taste if you let it stand in the chicken. And be sure to store separately any leftover stuffing; don't refrigerate it inside the chicken.

SAVORY STUFFING

Makes 2 cups.

1/2 cup chopped celery leaves
2 tablespoons chopped onion
4 tablespoons (1/2 stick) butter or margarine
1/2 cup water
2 cups ready-mix bread stuffing (1/2 of an 8-ounce package)

1. Sauté celery leaves and onion in butter or margarine in medium-size saucepan. Add water; heat to boiling.
2. Stir in bread stuffing; toss with fork just until moistened.

HOW MUCH STUFFING?

Stuffing swells as it cooks. Some people allow a cup of plain stuffing for each pound of chicken, but if you're using a rich stuffing, ½ cup stuffing per pound of chicken should be enough. Remember too that if you have unused stuffing after you have filled your chicken (or chickens), you can put the extra stuffing in a baking dish and cook it for a delicious side dish.

HAWAIIAN STUFFING

Makes about 2½ cups.

1½ cups soft bread crumbs
1/3 cup flaked coconut
1/4 cup finely chopped celery
1/4 cup drained, crushed pineapple
1 tablespoon grated orange peel
2 tablespoons melted butter or margarine

Combine all ingredients in a bowl and toss lightly to blend.

FRUIT STUFFING

Makes 7 cups.

1 can (pound) sliced apples
Water
1/2 cup (1 stick) butter or margarine
1 package (2 cups) ready-mix bread stuffing
1 cup chopped peanuts
1/2 cup seedless raisins

1. Drain apples and add water to apple liquid to make 1 cup. Heat to boiling in large saucepan.
2. Stir in butter or margarine until melted.
3. Add ready-mix stuffing, apples, peanuts, and raisins, tossing lightly to mix.

BREAD-AND-BUTTER STUFFING

Makes about 3 cups.

3 cups (about 6 slices) small dry bread
  cubes. To make dry bread cubes: spread
  cubes out on baking sheet; bake in a very
  slow oven (300°) 15 minutes, or until
  cubes are dry but not brown.
1 small onion, finely chopped ($^1/_4$ cup)
2 tablespoons chopped parsley
$1^1/_2$ teaspoons crumbled basil
$^1/_4$ teaspoon salt
$^1/_8$ teaspoon pepper
1 egg
$^1/_4$ cup ($^1/_2$ stick) melted butter or margarine

1. Combine bread cubes, onion, parsley, basil, salt, pepper, and egg in medium-size bowl.
2. Sprinkle melted butter or margarine over bread mixture; toss with fork until blended.

HILO STUFFING

Makes 4 cups.

1 cup uncooked white rice
4 tablespoons ($^1/_2$ stick) butter or margarine
1 medium-size onion, chopped ($^1/_2$ cup)
2 envelopes instant chicken broth
  OR 2 chicken bouillon cubes
$2^1/_2$ cups water
$^1/_2$ cup chopped macadamia nuts
  (from a 6-ounce jar)
$^1/_2$ cup flaked coconut

1. In a large saucepan, sauté rice in butter or margarine, stirring often, just until golden.
2. Stir in onion, chicken broth or bouillon cubes, and water; heat to boiling, crushing cubes, if using, with a spoon; cover. Simmer 20 minutes, or until rice is tender and liquid is absorbed.
3. Sprinkle with nuts and coconut; toss lightly to mix.

GOURMET STUFFING

Makes 2 cups.

3 chicken livers
4 tablespoons ($^1/_2$ stick) butter or margarine
2 cups soft bread crumbs (4 slices)
2 tablespoons chopped onion
1 tablespoon water
1 teaspoon Worcestershire sauce
$^1/_2$ teaspoon salt

1. Sauté chicken livers in butter or margarine, stirring often, in small frying pan 5 minutes, or until livers lose their pink color.
2. Remove livers and chop, then add to bread crumbs in medium-sized bowl. Sauté onion just until soft in same frying pan.
3. Stir water, Worcestershire sauce, and salt into onions into frying pan; pour over crumb mixture. Toss lightly to mix well. (Mixture will be crumbly, not wet.)

APRICOT-WALNUT STUFFING

Makes 4 cups.

1 medium-size onion, chopped ($^1/_2$ cup)
4 tablespoons ($^1/_2$ stick) butter or margarine
$^1/_2$ cup chopped dry apricots
1 envelope instant chicken broth
  OR 1 chicken bouillon cube
$^1/_3$ cup water
6 slices white bread, cubed (about 3 cups)
$^1/_2$ cup chopped walnuts

1. In a large frying pan, sauté onion in butter or margarine until soft; stir in apricots, chicken broth or bouillon cube, and water. Heat to boiling, crushing bouillon cube if used; remove from heat.
2. Add cubed bread and walnuts; toss until evenly moist.

GRAVIES, SAUCES, GLAZES

A dollop of something delicious can go a long way toward dressing up a chicken. Milk gravy spooned over simple fried chicken, cream giblet gravy with a fine roast, dark cherry sauce ladled over broiled chicken — all serve to enhance the meat's inherent goodness. And a luscious tangy glaze — applied to a chicken while it cooks — not only lends taste but adds a golden gloss. Here is a collection of gravies, sauces, and glazes that can be served with most any plainly prepared chicken; a few others can be found with the chicken recipes they belong to and will be listed in the INDEX.

CREAM GIBLET GRAVY

Makes about 2½ cups.

Chicken giblets, back, and neck
1½ cups plus 2 tablespoons water
1 small onion, sliced
2 tablespoons flour
1 cup evaporated milk
Salt and pepper

1. Combine giblets (except liver), back, neck, 1½ cups water, and onion in medium-size saucepan; cover.
2. Simmer 1 hour, or until tender. Add liver about 20 minutes before end of cooking time.
3. Remove giblets and chicken pieces (reserve broth); cool; dice giblets and any small pieces of meat; save for Step 5.
4. Strain broth, adding water if needed to make 1 cup. Return broth to saucepan; stir in flour blended to a smooth paste with 2 tablespoons water.
5. Cook over low heat, stirring constantly, until gravy thickens and boils 1 minute; stir in evaporated milk and chopped giblets and chicken; season to taste with salt and pepper.

BROWN GRAVY

Makes 1 cup.

	Thick	Thin
Fat (from pan meat was cooked in)	**2 tbls.**	**1 tbls.**
Flour	**2 tbls.**	**1 tbls.**
Liquid from cooked meat plus water or stock, if needed	**1 cup**	**1 cup**
Salt and pepper	**to taste**	**to taste**

1. Pour all liquid from pan into measuring cup (fat will rise to top); skim off fat; return to pan measured amount of fat needed; save liquid for Step 4.
2. Blend flour and fat in pan.
3. Place pan over low heat; stir, scraping bottom of pan to loosen meat pieces, until fat-flour mixture is richly browned.
4. Remove from heat; gradually stir in measured liquid.
5. Cook over low heat, stirring constantly, until gravy thickens and boils 1 minute.
6. Season to taste; color with bottled gravy coloring, if you wish.
7. Strain gravy; spoon some around meat; pass remaining in bowl.

MILK GRAVY

Makes 2 cups.

2 tablespoons butter or margarine
2 tablespoons flour
1 cup milk
1 teaspoon meat-extract paste dissolved in
   1 cup hot water
Salt and pepper

1. Melt butter or margarine in small saucepan; remove from heat.
2. Blend in flour; stir in milk and meat-extract paste dissolved in hot water.
3. Cook, stirring constantly, until mixture thickens and boils 1 minute; season to taste. Serve hot.

CREAM GRAVY

Makes 2 cups.

Melt 2 tablespoons chicken fat, butter, or margarine in small saucepan; remove from heat. Blend in 2 tablespoons flour; stir in 1 cup light cream and 1 cup strained chicken broth (or use 1 chicken bouillon cube dissolved in 1 cup hot water). Cook, stirring constantly, until gravy thickens and boils 1 minute; season to taste.

QUICK CREAM GRAVY

Makes about 1½ cups.

Blend ¼ cup evaporated milk into 1 can (10 ounces) chicken gravy in small saucepan. Heat slowly, stirring constantly, until bubbly-hot and smooth.

PAN GRAVY

Makes 1¼ cups.

Blend 2 tablespoons drippings from chicken with 2 tablespoons flour, 1 tablespoon brown sugar, and ½ teaspoon salt; stir in 1¼ cups water. Cook, stirring constantly until gravy thickens and boils 1 minute.

SAVORY MUSHROOM GRAVY

Makes about 2 cups.

Pour off all chicken drippings from pan chicken cooked in; return ¼ cupful. Stir in 1 can dry cream of mushroom soup mix. Blend in 2 cups water. Cook slowly, stirring constantly, 8 to 10 minutes, or until thickened.

HAWAIIAN BARBECUE SAUCE

Makes 1¾ cups.

1 cup pineapple juice
¼ cup soy sauce
¼ cup vinegar
¼ cup salad oil
½ teaspoon ground ginger
1 tablespoon sugar

1. Combine ingredients well.
2. Brush on broiler-fryer halves or quarters frequently until they are done.

PLUM SAUCE

Makes about 1 cup.

1 cup plum jam
1 tablespoon cider vinegar
1 teaspoon grated onion
½ teaspoon ground allspice
¼ teaspoon ground ginger

Combine all ingredients in a small saucepan; heat slowly, stirring constantly, to boiling. Cool.

MAKE-AHEAD NOTE: This sauce is a good keeper and may be made several days ahead and stored, covered, in the refrigerator. Let stand to warm before serving.

BARBECUE SAUCE

Makes 2½ cups.

2 cans (8 ounces each) tomato sauce
1 medium-size onion, chopped (½ cup)
1 clove garlic, minced
¼ cup soy sauce
2 tablespoons sugar
1 teaspoon dry mustard
⅛ teaspoon cayenne pepper

Mix all ingredients in a medium-size bowl.

DARK CHERRY SAUCE

Makes about 2 cups.

1 can (1 pound) pitted dark sweet cherries
2 tablespoons cornstarch
1 tablespoon prepared mustard
1 tablespoon molasses
Few drops red-pepper seasoning
Dash of salt
3 tablespoons lemon juice

1. Drain syrup from cherries into a 2-cup measure; add water to make 1½ cups. (Save cherries for Step 3.)
2. Blend a few tablespoons syrup into cornstarch until smooth in a small saucepan; stir in remaining syrup, mustard, molasses, red-pepper seasoning, and salt. Cook over low heat, stirring constantly, until mixture thickens and boils 3 minutes.
3. Stir in cherries and lemon juice; heat slowly just until bubbly. Serve hot.

MORNAY SAUCE

Makes about 1¼ cups.

2 tablespoons butter or margarine
2 tablespoons flour
¹/₂ teaspoon salt
¹/₈ teaspoon pepper
¹/₂ cup milk
¹/₂ cup chicken stock
³/₄ cup grated sharp Cheddar cheese
¹/₂ teaspoon prepared mustard
¹/₂ teaspoon Worcestershire sauce
1 tablespoon chopped parsley

1. Melt butter or margarine in small saucepan; remove from heat.
2. Blend in flour, salt, and pepper; stir in milk and chicken stock.
3. Cook over low heat, stirring constantly, until sauce thickens and boils 1 minute.
4. Add cheese, mustard, and Worcestershire sauce; continue cooking, stirring occasionally, until cheese melts; remove from heat.
5. Stir in parsley. Serve hot.

DOUBLE ORANGE GLAZE

Makes about ¾ cup.

Combine ½ cup thawed frozen concentrated orange juice (from a 6-ounce can), ¼ cup orange marmalade, and 2 tablespoons bottled meat sauce in a small saucepan. Heat slowly, stirring constantly until marmalade melts and mixture is blended; remove from heat.

GOLDEN PINEAPPLE GLAZE

Makes about ¾ cup.

Combine ¼ cup pineapple syrup, ¼ cup orange juice, 2 tablespoons bottled meat sauce, 1 tablespoon melted butter.

GINGER-HONEY GLAZE

Makes about ¾ cup.

Combine ½ cup soy sauce, 6 tablespoons honey, and 2 teaspoons ground ginger in small saucepan. Heat, stirring constantly, just to boiling.

CURRY-FRUIT GLAZE

Makes 2 cups.

8 slices bacon, diced
1 large onion, chopped (1 cup)
2 tablespoons flour
1 tablespoon curry powder
1 tablespoon sugar
1 teaspoon salt
1 teaspoon bottled steak sauce
2 envelopes instant beef broth
  OR 2 beef bouillon cubes
1 cup water
3 tablespoons lemon juice
1 jar (about 4 ounces) baby-pack strained
  apples-and-apricots

1. Fry bacon slowly in medium-size saucepan just until fat starts to cook out; stir in chopped onion; sauté just until soft.
2. Blend in flour, curry powder, sugar, salt, and steak sauce until mixture bubbles; stir in remaining ingredients. Heat, stirring constantly, to boiling, then simmer, uncovered, 15 minutes to thicken.

WINES TO SERVE
WITH CHICKEN

Wine adds a festive touch to any chicken meal, and half the fun is knowing that the wine you choose is the right wine for the meal you are serving. A few good rules are:

- Dishes full of taste seem to demand *full, rich wines,* such as those from the Rhône or Burgundy regions of France. These wines reach their peak when they are 6 years or older.
- Dishes delicate in flavor call for *light wines,* usually white, rosé, or young red wines such as Beaujolais. White wines taste best when they are about 2 years old. Light red wines should be about 4 years old, except Beaujolais, which should be drunk when they are as young as possible.

The best way to go about selecting wine is to have a list of light wines — white or red — and a list of full wines, mostly red. So here they are, country by country:

FULL WINES

For barbecued chicken, hearty chicken stews, full-flavored casseroles and baked dishes, and chicken with zesty sauces or spicy glazes:

California Reds
Zinfandel
Pinot Noir
Cabernet Sauvignon

Italian Reds
Chianti
Barolo

French Reds
Bordeaux (such as St.-Emilion or
 Pomerol)
Burgundy (such as Nuits-St.-Georges,
 Vosne-Romanée, Clos de Vougeot,
 Chambolle-Musigny, Morey-St.-
 Denis, Gevrey-Chambertin, Fixin)
Rhône (such as Châteauneuf-du-Pape
 or Hermitage)

French Whites
Rhône (Hermitage Blanc)

Alsatian Whites
Sylvaner, Traminer, Gewürztraminer

LIGHT WINES

For fried chicken, broiled chicken, simple roasts, lightly flavored stews and pies, and such cold chicken dishes as salads and sandwiches:

California Whites
Mountain White
Pinot Blanc
Gray Riesling
Pinot Chardonnay
Johannisberger Riesling

California Reds
Mountain Red

German Whites
Liebfraumilch
Steinwein
Moselblümchen
Mosel (one from Graach or Bernkastel)
Rheinpfalz (one from Ruppertsberg or Forst)
Rheinhessen (one from Oppenheim or Nierstein)
Rheingau (one from Eltville or Erbach)

Italian Whites
Verdicchio
Orvieto
Soave

Italian Reds
Bardolino
Valpolicella

French Whites
Loire (such as Pouilly-Fumé or Muscadet)
Alsace (such as Pinot Gris or Riesling)
Bordeaux (such as Graves)
Burgundy (such as Pouilly-Fuissé or Meursault)
(*Note:* a white Burgundy such as Chablis, while too dry for most chicken, is excellent with pâtés, chicken liver dishes, and dishes or stuffings that include shellfish.)

French Reds
Rhône (such as Côtes du Rhône)
Burgundy (such as Beaujolais, Côtes de Beaune-Villages, Chassagne-Montrachet, Volnay, Pommard, Santenay, Beaune, Monthélie)
Bordeaux (such as Graves, Médoc, Haut-Médoc)

PINK WINES
Many people prefer pink wines to accompany Oriental or lightly-flavored chicken dishes. Good choices are rosés from Anjou or Portugal.

SHERRY
With chicken appetizers and soups, a dry chilled sherry is delicious, especially one called Fino or Manzanilla. Sherry is also the drink to serve when your chicken dish has sherry in the sauce.

CHAMPAGNE
The all-purpose wine champagne can accompany any chicken dish. When served with food, a "sec" (dry) usually tastes better than one labeled "brut," which is very very dry.

A chicken in your shopping cart means the start of a good meal at a low price. If you compare what each dollar of your meat budget will buy, you will find that economically chicken is hard to beat. For variety of choice, ways to cook, nutrition, and popularity, it rates at the top too. It is also easily available in any season. One reason for this is the fact that today chicken-raising is big business.

Our modern birds are a pampered lot. They are scientifically bred and fed nutritionally correct foods to make them plump and juicy. Efficient processing and speedy refrigerated transportation guarantee users a carefully controlled quality food. The chickens you buy are mass-produced for their meat; the popular broiler-fryer differs from egg-producing chickens the way beef cattle differs from dairy cows. While it used to take months to raise a chicken for market, it now takes just weeks, and the savings show up in the price at your supermarket. No wonder we now eat about five times as much chicken as we did twenty years ago.

The term "spring chicken" is disappearing from our vocabulary, because chickens are now available in prime quality at any season. They are *fed* their Vitamin D and don't need to get it all from the warm sunshine anymore.

Name your choice

Because of the wide variety of chickens available, it is a good idea to know something about the different types.

Top preference among homemakers seems to be the broiler-fryer, a small, young chicken that has been bred to homemaker specifications. You can buy this chicken whole, split, quartered, or cut up in serving-size pieces. You can even buy certain parts alone — breasts, thighs and drumsticks, or wings — if your family especially likes white or dark meat, or if you wish to make a recipe that calls for parts. In the supermarkets, chicken comes tray-packed in all these forms. Cleaned whole birds also come in bags of two, three, or more, ready for cooking or to cut up at home, as you wish.

Broiler-fryers can be used for most any chicken dish — to fry, broil, barbecue, even roast. Other good choices of chicken are plump roasters weighing 3½ to 5 pounds, and large meaty hens — sometimes referred to as "bro-hens" — which are good to fricassee or simmer juicy-tender for chicken pie, stew, salad, or casserole.

Check this list of chicken types in planning your menus:

broiler-fryer: The all-purpose meat chicken; may be cooked by any method. A broiler-fryer is young (about 9 weeks old) and weighs 1½ to 3½ pounds.

roaster: Slightly larger and older than a broiler-fryer; weighs 3½ to 5 pounds and is about 12 weeks old.

Rock Cornish hen: A very young, very small chicken (weighing 1½ pounds or less); usually served roasted — one to a person.

stewing chicken or bro-hen: A plump meaty bird usually a little over a year old and weighing about 4½ to 6 pounds. Good for kettle dishes, soups, and salads.

capon: A young, plump, large, de-sexed rooster with much white meat and a fine flavor; weighs about 4 to 7 pounds and is most often roasted.

pullet: An old-fashioned term for a young chicken, rarely used in today's recipes.

Shopping for chicken

Besides the many kinds of fresh chicken available, you can also buy this fowl frozen and canned. Take your pick. Fresh chicken is best for same-day or next-day cooking; frozen, to put away in your freezer; canned, to keep on your shelf, ready when you need it in a hurry.

The kind of fresh chicken you choose depends on how you want to cook it. Your family may prefer light or dark meat, or you may want special parts for a special dish. (Because they save fixing time and give you exactly what you want with no waste, chicken parts are often your thriftiest buys.)

Buy by brand name, government inspection mark and grade, or the stamp of your favorite dependable supermarket. By federal law, all ready-to-cook fresh poultry from another state, as well as frozen and canned chicken, is inspected for cleanliness and marked with a circle stamp "Inspected for wholesomeness by U.S. Department of Agriculture." Most states have some inspection laws of their own that apply to the processing of chickens sold within the state. Some plants also ask for grade or quality rating, which is not required by law; the grade mark is in the form of a shield and says "USDA Grade A" on it. (There are two lower grades, Grade B and Grade C, but you will practically never see a label with those grades printed on them.) Often the inspection circle and grade shield appear together on a tag attached to the chicken.

Watch for specials on chicken, then buy some for today's dinner and some for the freezer. Remember to cook ahead when you can — it takes little work to fry a big batch of parts at once, or to put a second bird in to roast, or to stew an extra chicken for another day's meal.

How much to buy

Here are some rules to follow in deciding how much to buy, although you may want to increase these portions for big eaters in your family:

Chicken for frying
   Allow ¾ pound to 1 pound per serving
Chicken for roasting
   Allow ¾ pound to 1 pound per serving
Chicken for broiling or barbecuing
   Allow ½ chicken or 1 pound per serving
Rock Cornish hens
   Allow 1 per person
Chicken for stewing
   Allow ½ pound to 1 pound per serving

Count on about 1 cup of cut-up cooked meat from each 1 pound of uncooked stewing chicken. You will need more when making a salad, or slicing for sandwiches and cold cuts, than when fixing a casserole or creamed dish.

HOW TO STORE AND FREEZE CHICKEN

Fresh chicken

Chicken is perishable — the minute you get home from the supermarket, unwrap packaged chicken from its transparent plastic wrap, and remove giblets (the edible innards — heart, gizzard, liver) which come separately wrapped in a little package. Rewrap chicken lightly in wax paper, foil, or transparent wrap, and place it in the meat compartment or on the coldest shelf of your refrigerator. It will keep for one or two days. Store giblets separately and cook as soon as possible, within 24 hours.

If you wish to freeze fresh chicken, unwrap it from its transparent wrap (again, do this as soon as you get home), discard the backing board or tray, and rinse (don't soak) the chicken in cold running water. Pat dry, then wrap the clean bird tightly in transparent wrap, foil, or freezer paper, and place it in your freezer. It will keep 2 or 3 months. Never freeze an uncooked *stuffed* chicken; the stuffing will sour.

Frozen chicken

Hard-frozen chicken may go right from your shopping cart into your freezer without rewrapping. But do not allow it to thaw at all. If for any reason the frozen chicken you bought has thawed, cook it promptly and *then* freeze it, if you wish. Never refreeze chicken.

Should frozen chicken be thawed before cooking? If you are making stew, the chicken can go into the kettle frozen. But for frying, broiling, barbe-cuing, or roasting, it is better to thaw the chicken first, because it cooks more evenly that way. The best way to defrost chicken is to take it out of the freezer a day or two ahead and put it into the refrigerator. Don't unwrap it, because the skin tends to dry and toughen when exposed to air. You can hasten thawing by placing the chicken, still in its freezer wrap, under cold running water. Once it is thawed, don't lose time in cooking it.

Cooked chicken

Chicken that has been cooked ahead for a meal to be eaten during the next day or two can be kept, covered, in a colder part of the refrigerator. Leftover chicken similarly can be placed in a covered container immediately after the meal and kept in the refrigerator for 2 or 3 days. Refrigerate broth or gravy in separate covered containers. Remove any stuffing from stuffed birds and store that separately too. Use within a couple of days.

Cooked chicken can go into your freezer cooled and tightly wrapped and can be kept for a month before serving. In freezing leftover roast chicken you should transfer it from refrigerator to freezer within 24 hours after roasting. It will save space to cut away meat from the bones first (you have no future use for the carcass) and freeze only the meat. Wrap in transparent freezer wrap or aluminum foil, label with amount (cup measure or number of slices), date. Use within a month.

HOW TO CUT UP CHICKEN

1. Place chicken on its back on a cutting board. Grasp one leg and lift it away from the body of the chicken, and cut through joint close to back. Repeat with other leg.

2. Cut through each leg joint to separate thigh from drumstick.

3. Pull wing out from body and cut through joint close to body. Remove other wing same way.

4. Separate breast section from back in one large piece by cutting along ribs on each side. Split breast section down middle, or bone it.

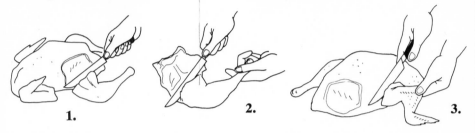

HOW TO BONE CHICKEN BREASTS

1. Place chicken breast, skin side down, on a cutting board. With a knife, cut just through the white gristle at the neck end of the keel bone (the dark bone that runs down the center of the breast). Bend the breast back and press flat with your hands to expose the keel bone. Loosen the keel bone by running the tip of your index finger around both sides; remove it in one or two pieces.

2. Insert the tip of the knife under the long rib bone on one side of the breast. Work the knife underneath the bone and cut the bone free from the meat. Lifting the bone away from the breast, cut the meat from the rib cage, cutting around the outer edge of the breast up to the shoulder joint, and then through the joint. This removes entire rib cage. Repeat procedure on other side.

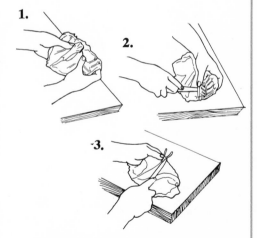

3. Now working from the ends of the wishbone, scrape the flesh away from each piece of bone; cut out the bone. Slip the knife underneath the white tendons on each side of the breast to loosen them, and pull them out.

HOW TO STUFF AND TRUSS A CHICKEN

First rinse chicken completely clean with cold running water inside and out. Pat dry. Rub the cavity lightly with salt.

1. Spoon stuffing lightly into neck (do not pack, for stuffing expands when cooking). Pull neck skin over the opening and fasten to back with a skewer or toothpick.

2. Stuff body cavity lightly. Close the opening by running skewers or toothpicks through the skin from one side of the opening to the other; then lace securely with string in a crisscross fashion. Or, you can sew the opening closed with a large needle and thread.

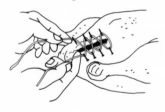

3. Loop the same string around the drumstick ends and tie them together, then fasten them to the tailpiece.

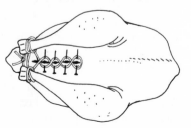

4. Fold wings up and over the back; this will help brace the chicken in the roasting pan. Brush chicken lightly with melted butter or margarine and place, breast up, in a roasting pan.

Or, if barbecuing on a spit:

4. Press wings close to breast and run a string around under the chicken to completely encircle it, securing the wings snugly against the breast. The chicken should be tied so it makes a compact bundle.

OVEN ROASTING TIMETABLE

Chicken weight (ready to cook)	Oven temp.	Roasting time
Under 1½ pounds	400°	1 to 1½ hours
1½ to 3½ pounds	375°	1¼ to 1¾ hours
3½ to 5 pounds	375°	1¾ to 2¼ hours
5 to 8 pounds	375°	2 to 4 hours

HOW TO CARVE CHICKEN

To carve roast chicken you need first of all a good, sharp, thin-bladed knife, and a sharp long-tined fork. Keep your carving equipment in good condition, and do not use it for any purposes other than what it was intended for.

Before you begin to carve, be sure you remove from the chicken all the trussing equipment — skewers, toothpicks, cord, or thread.

Place the chicken breast-up on a serving platter or carving board large enough to make handling easy. You might have a separate plate nearby to hold drumsticks and wings out of the way as you remove them.

1. Place platter square in front of you, the chicken on its back with its legs toward your right. Grasping end of leg nearest you, bend it down toward platter while you cut through thigh joint to separate whole leg from body. Separate drumstick and thigh by cutting through joint.

2. Stick fork into breast near breastbone and cut off wing close to body. Slanting knife inward slightly may make it easier to hit the joint.

3. Slice white meat, starting at tip of breastbone and cutting down toward wing joint. Repeat with other side of chicken, turning platter if you wish.

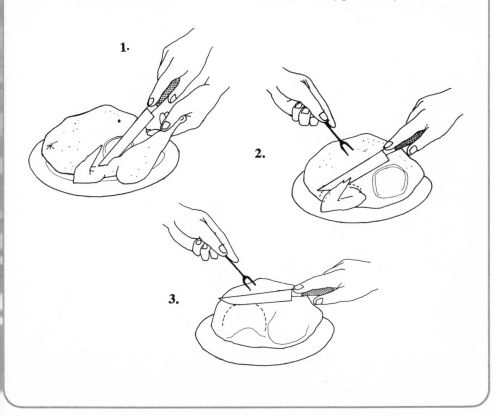

INDEX

160